Introduction

The primary aim of the Primary Mathematics curriculum is to allow students to develop their ability in mathematical problem solving. This includes using and applying mathematics in practical, real-life situation as well as within the discipline of mathematics itself. Therefore, this curriculum covers a wide range of situations from routine problems to problems in unfamiliar contexts to open-ended investigations that make use of relevant mathematical concepts.

One of the means to develop mathematical problem solving is to teach a student how to use what information he or she already has to solve something new. For example, instead of simply teaching addition and subtraction facts to 20 after the student learns the facts to 10, this curriculum teaches the student how to use the facts they already know for addition and subtraction within 10 to add and subtract larger numbers within 20. Then those skills are used to add and subtract numbers within 40, while learning a few more skills. These are then used to add and subtract within 100. Students do memorize addition and subtraction facts within 20, but understanding the place-value system and developing a number sense that can be used to figure out these facts comes first.

The problems in the textbook do not focus on practicing a procedure as much as on applying the concepts. The textbook and the workbook are a basis for developing mathematical reasoning skills. Practicing a procedure can be easily added through additional worksheets for students who need more practice. As you go through this curriculum, it is important that you gauge your own student's understanding of concepts and need for additional practice and provide it, rather than simply moving from one page to the next page and assuming that everything for every student can be accomplished with little input on your part as an parent/instructor.

An important feature of learning mathematics with this curriculum is the use of a concrete introduction to the concept, followed by a pictorial representation, followed by the abstract symbols. The textbook supplies the pictorial and abstract aspects of this progression. You, as the instructor, should supply the concrete introduction. You can also move into a pictorial aspect before even using the textbook. If the topic is new to the student, provide the concrete introduction before doing the tasks in the text. Use the tasks in the textbook more as an assessment of understanding. If the topic is mostly review, you can use concrete objects if you detect some misunderstanding. For some students a concrete illustration is more important than for other students. As you teach your child, you can gauge his or her understanding of the material, and compensate as necessary. No curriculum can provide that personal and necessary part of instruction.

The format of the textbook is different from other texts that you may be used to in that it is organized more like a book with chapters and subchapters, rather than into well-defined lessons all using the same number of pages followed by the same number of problems. The textbook is meant to be used for discussion, learning, and assessment with the teacher. You should use the textbook as an activity book that you do with your student as part of the lesson. Some pages or tasks are meant for discussion that can go beyond the obvious answer. Other tasks are straightforward ones where you student simple supplies the answer. If you have preceded the use of the textbook with teaching activities, you can use these tasks for assessment of your student's understanding. The workbook is for independent practice.

The purpose of this guide is to help you to understand the important concepts of the *Primary Mathematics 1* curriculum, to gain an understanding of how these concepts fit in with the program as a whole, to provide suggestions to help you to introduce concepts concretely and use the textbook effectively, and to provide suggestions for additional activities for reinforcement and practice. Pick and choose the activities that are most useful for your particular student – you do not have to do every activity. Ideally, you would do some of the teaching activities as a concrete introduction to the topic, then do the textbook pages with your child, and then do the reinforcement activities when or as needed.

This guide will give you a suggested amount of time in weeks to spend on each unit. It does not provide daily lessons. Since you are working with one or a few students, you have the opportunity to spend as much or as little time as needed on a particular concept. For some units, your child may be able to do the work more quickly, and for others more slowly. Take the time your student needs on each topic. There is plenty of time for additional practice. One "lesson" in the guide can take 1-3 days, depending on your child. For example, if one lesson has 2 workbook exercises, you can take 2 days, using reinforcement activities the second day.

The following page has a suggested weekly schedule, along with objectives for each lesson.

Scheme of Work

Week		Objectives	Text book	Work book	Guide
Unit 1: Numbers 0 to 10					
		Part 1: Counting			1
1	1	▪ Count to 10, read and write numerals and number words. ▪ Recognize 0 as an empty set.	6-11	7-10	2-3
	2	▪ Compare numbers within 10. ▪ Understand "more" and "less".	12-13	11-12	4-5
	3	▪ Count on from some number to 10. ▪ Count backward from 10 to 1. ▪ Find one more or one less than a number within 10. ▪ Arrange the numbers 1-10 in order. ▪ Determine missing numbers in a sequence.	14-15	13-14	6
Unit 2: Number Bonds					
		Part 1: Making Number Stories			7-9
2	1	▪ Make up number stories to illustrate number bonds. ▪ Associate number bonds with part-whole. ▪ Divide groups up in different ways. ▪ Find and memorize number pairs that make 2, 3, 4, 5, and 6.	16-18	15	10-11
	2	▪ Find and memorize number pairs that make 7. ▪ Find and memorize number pairs that make 8. ▪ Find and memorize number pairs that make 9. ▪ Find and memorize number pairs that make 10.	19-21	16-19	12-14
3	3	▪ Find the missing part of a number bond.	22	20-22	15-16
	4	▪ Review ways to make 10.	23	23-24	17-18

Week		Objectives	Text book	Work book	Guide
Unit 3: Addition					
		Part 1: Making Addition Stories			19
4	1	▪ Understand the meaning of addition. ▪ Make number stories for addition.	24	25-27	20-21
	2	▪ Write addition equations using "+" and "=". ▪ Write several addition equations for a given story.	25-29	28-30	22-23
		Part 2: Addition with Number Bonds			24-25
	1	▪ Relate addition stories to number bonds. ▪ Write two addition facts for a given number bond.	30-31	31-35	26
	2	▪ Solve picture problems using addition. ▪ Memorize addition facts through 5, +0, +1.	32	35-37	27
		Part 3: Other Methods of Addition			28-29
5	1	▪ Count on to add 1, 2, or 3 to a number. ▪ Learn facts for +2, +3.	33-35	38-39	30-31
	2	▪ Learn facts for making 10. ▪ Learn facts for 3 + 4, 4 + 5. ▪ Review addition facts through 10.	36-37	40	32-33
Unit 4: Subtraction					
		Part 1: Making Subtraction Stories			34
6	1	▪ Understand the meaning of subtraction. ▪ Make number stories for subtraction.	38	41-44	35-36
	2	▪ Write subtraction equations using "−" and "=". ▪ Write several subtraction equations for a given situation.	39-43	45-47	37
		Part 2: Methods of Subtraction			38-41
	1	▪ Relate subtraction facts within 10 to the missing part of a number bond. ▪ Write two subtraction facts for a given number bond.	44-46	48-51	42

Week		Objectives	Text book	Work book	Guide
	2	• Write two addition equations and two subtraction equations for a given number bond.	47	52-55	43-44
7	3	• Count back to subtract 1, 2, or 3 from a number within 10. • Memorize subtraction facts for −0, −1, −2, −3.	48-49	56-57	45-46
	4	• Recognize numbers that differ by 1 or 2. • Count on to subtract numbers close to each other. • Subtract from 10.	50	58	47-48
8	5	• Review addition and subtraction within 10.	51	59	49
	6	• Interpret addition and subtraction stories.		60-65	50-51
Unit 5: Ordinal Numbers					
		Part 1: Naming Positions			52
9	1	• Name a position using ordinal numbers 1st through 10th. • Find an ordinal position from the left or from the right.	52-53	66-70	53-54
Review					
		• Review all topics.		71-82	55
Unit 6: Numbers to 20					
		Part 1: Counting and Comparing			56-57
10	1	• Count to 20 by building up from 10. • Read and write numerals and number words for 11 to 19.	54-56	83-87	58-59
	2	• Relate numbers 11 to 20 to a ten + ones.	57-58	88-89	60
	3	• Count backwards from 20. • Determine missing numbers in a sequence from 1 to 20.	58-59	90-91	61
	4	• Compare and order numbers within 20.	60-61	92-94	62-63

Week		Objectives	Text book	Work book	Guide
		Part 2: Addition and Subtraction			64-65
11	1	▪ Add 1-digit numbers whose sum is greater than 10 by first making a ten.	62-64	95-98	66-68
	2	▪ Add a 1-digit number to a 2-digit number within 20 (no renaming) by adding ones.	65	99-101	69
12	3	▪ Subtract a 1-digit number from a 2-digit number within 20 when there are enough ones (no renaming).	65-66	102-104	70-71
	4	▪ Subtract a 1-digit number from a 2-digit number within 20 when there are not enough ones by subtracting from the ten.	66	105-107	72-74
	5	▪ Add 1, 2, or 3 to a number within 20 by counting on. ▪ Subtract 1, 2, or 3 from a number within 20 by counting back.	67	108-109	75
13	6	▪ Write a family of two addition and two subtraction equations for a given fact. ▪ Practice basic addition and subtraction facts within 20.		110-115	76-77
Review					
		▪ Review all topics.		116-123	78
Unit 7: Shapes					
		Part 1: Common Shapes			79
14	1	▪ Recognize and name the four basic shapes: circle, triangle, square, and rectangle.	68-70	124-129	80
	2	▪ Sort and classify objects by shape, size, color, or orientation.	71-73	130-134	81
	3	▪ Describe or continue a pattern according to one or two attributes such as shape, size, or color.	74-75	135-136	82-83
	4	▪ Choose suitable shapes to fit together to make a basic shape.	76-77	137	84

Manipulatives

It is important to introduce the concepts concretely, but it is not important exactly what manipulative is used. A few possible manipulatives are suggested here. The linking cubes and playing cards will be used at many levels of the *Primary Mathematics*.

Multilink cubes or Connect-a-Cubes
These are cubes that can be linked together on all 6 sides. Ten of them can be connected to form tens so that you have tens and ones. You can use Lego's™ or anything else that can be grouped into tens, but the multilink cubes will be useful when the students get to volume problems in *Primary Mathematics* 4.

Four sets of cards:
You can use index cards to make them, but use crayon or pencil rather than marker so the numbers don't show through on the back side. Ideally, use blank playing cards. You can also copy the cards in the appendix, ideally onto cardstock, and cut them out.

➢ Set 1: Numerals 0-20. Include one longer card for 10 so that, when teaching numbers from 10 to 19, you can slide the single digits over the 10 card.
➢ Set 2: Number words one to twenty
➢ Set 3: Dot cards for 0-10. You can use index cards and trace around pennies, or use dot stickers that are available as office supply. Have cards with 1, 2, 3, 4, or 5 down one side for the numbers 1-5, cards with 5 down one side and 1, 2, 3, 4, or 5 down the other side for numbers 6-10. Make some extra ones for 10.
➢ Set 4: Dot cards similar to set 3, but cards showing doubles for 2, 3, and 4 (the example here is for double 3), and cards showing doubles + 1 (add another dot to one of the rows showing double 3 to show 3 + 4).
➢ Set 5: Dot cards for "making 10". Put 10 empty circles on each card, 5 on each side, and color in 1, 2, 3, 4, 5, 6, 7, 8, or 9 circles, going down one side before the other. (The example here is for 7.)

Counters
Round counters are easy to use and pick up, and can be used for number discs later, but any type of counter will work.

Playing cards 0-10
You need four sets of number cards 0-10. You can use a deck of cards and call the ace 1. You can white-out the ace and replace it with a 1. Use the cards to play games that help your student memorize the math facts. You can whiteout the J on the Jack and call that a 0, or use the tens from another deck and whiteout the 1 of the 10 and all the symbols.

Fact cards
A set of addition and subtraction fact cards (for addition and subtraction within 10). These can have the fact on one side and the answer on the other for individual practice.
Fact game cards: Fact cards with answers on separate cards rather than on the back of the card with the addition fact.

Whiteboard and dry-erase markers
Many of the activities require use of a table-top. This guide does not assume you will be teaching in the same way as in a classroom, i.e. with a white board on the wall. Smaller whiteboards that can be used at the table, or by the student to work out problems on, instead of paper, are ideal.

Hundred-chart
Make one or buy one with squares large enough to cover with counters or coins. There is one in the appendix that can be copied.

Number cubes or dice
Some of the games or activities use number cubes. You can get blank cubes with labels, or simply label regular dice using masking tape. Several 10-sided dice are handy for games and activities, but not required.

Simple balance

Supplements

The textbook and workbook provide the essence of the math curriculum. Some students profit by additional practice, more review. Other students profit by more challenging problems. There are several workbooks keyed to the Primary Mathematics series that can be used for this. More information about these can be found at www.singaporemath.com. If you feel it is important that your student have a lot of drill in math facts, there are many websites that generate worksheets according to your specifications, or provide on-line fact practice. Web sites come and go, but doing a search using the terms "math fact practice" will turn up many sites. Playing simple card games is another way to practice math facts.

Unit 1 – Numbers 0 to 10

Part 1 – Counting

Before starting *Primary Mathematics*, most students have already been counting and using numbers beyond 10 in daily situations, and can also read numerals (number symbols). Some students may also be able to read and write number words. Unit 1 is primarily meant to reinforce these skills.

Give your student plenty of practice writing the numerals, if necessary. Many students can write numerals but are not yet ready to spell number words at this age. It is up to you how much you want your child to be able to write and spell the number words correctly now. Writing number words is not a necessary skill at this point, and can be further practiced at other times in other contexts. Recognizing (reading) the number words, however, is helpful unless you are reading to your child.

In this unit, students are comparing sets of objects concretely and pictorially where they can count the objects in each set and match the objects in one set to the objects in the other set to see which set has more. You can wait until after the next section to ask your student to compare numerals abstractly; that is, without sets of objects. It is not necessary right now to get your student to tell you how many there are more or less in one set than the other. In *Primary Mathematics 2*, students will learn the symbols ">" and "<".

0, or "zero" stands for the empty set.

Most students already understand that numbers have order, and each number is one more than the previous number. Number order is reviewed in this unit.

Material

Objects to count
Numeral cards 0-10
Number word cards, one to ten
Dot cards 0-10
Counters
Multilink cubes
Playing cards 0-10

(1) Review counting, numerals, and number words

Textbook

Pages 6-9

Task 1, pp. 10-11

1. 4	1
0	3
2	5
10	
6	8
9	7

Workbook

Exercise 1

1. four one three five
   zero two
2. nine seven five six
   ten eight

Exercise 2

1. 4	7
10	5
9	6
2	8

2. Check that the correct amounts are colored.

Teaching activities

Ask your student to count sets of objects, such as counters, multilink cubes, toy cars, toy animals, chairs at the table, etc. Make sure she uses one-to-one correspondence; that is, counts one object for one number.

Give your student a set of number cards. Display a set of ten or less objects and ask him to select the correct number card.

Set out number cards and dot cards at random and ask your student to match them.

Put the number word cards in order and read them out loud to your student. Then ask her to read them along with you, then alone. Then mix them up and ask her to read them out loud.

Set out numeral cards and number word cards and ask your student to match them.

Discuss pages 6-9 in the textbook and have your student do task 1, pp. 10-11.

Reinforcement

Show numeral cards at random and ask your student to count out the correct number of counters.

Show numeral cards at random and ask your student to write the number words.

Show your student a set of objects and see if he can guess how many there are without counting.

Show number word cards at random and ask your student to say or write the numeral, or count out the correct number of counters.

Ask your student to make different dot patterns for a given number of dots. Some dot patterns for 7 are shown here.

Game: Go Fish variation:
Material: Numeral cards, number word cards, and dot cards. (This gives you a deck of 30 cards, including 0's.)
Goal: To make sets of all three cards for a number.
Procedure: Mix up the cards and deal out 5 cards to each player. Place the remaining cards face down in the center. The first player asks another player if he or she has a number that the first player is holding. For example, the player has a dot card for 6. He asks another player for all her sixes. If she has any sixes, she must give them all to him, and he can ask her or another player for cards. If she does not, she says "Go fish" (or other term), and he draws a card from the pile in the center. Then it is the next player's turn. When a player has a set of three cards, he or she puts them down face up.

(2) Review more and less, comparing numbers

Textbook

Tasks 2-5, pp. 12-13

2. (a) yes
   (b) no
   (c) no
4. The dolls
5. The butterflies

Workbook

Exercise 3

1. (a) 2nd and 4th
   (b) 1st and 4th
   (c) 2nd and 4th
   (d) 1st and 3rd
   (e) 1st and 4th
2. (a) glasses
   (b) mice
3. (a) flowers
   (b) heads

Teaching activities

Use two types of objects, such as two colors of counters or multilink cubes, or two types of toys.

Display two sets, one of each type of object with the same number of objects in each set, such as four objects.

Ask your student to count the number in each set. Ask him if the numbers are the same. They are.
Add one item to one of the sets.

Ask your student how many are in each set. Then ask her if both sets have the same number. They do not.

Ask which set has more. Lead your student to say:
There are more cars than planes.
5 is more than 4

Ask which set has less. Lead your student to say:
There are fewer planes than cars.
4 is less than 5.

Display two sets of objects, set out randomly. Ask your student to decide which set has more. He can line them up to see which set has more or less.

Repeat the above activity, but without letting your student move the objects around to line them up. You can either place the objects on paper so that she can draw lines between pairs of objects, or you can ask her to count the number of objects in each set.

Ask your student to do tasks 2-5, textbook pp. 12-13.

Reinforcement

Use playing cards 1- 10. Shuffle the cards and lay down the top two face up. Ask your student to tell you which number is larger.

Use numeral cards 1-10. Lay down pairs of numeral cards and ask your student which number is larger. This is more challenging than the previous activity, because the student can't look at objects to determine which is larger.

Game - "War"
Material: Playing cards 1-10. In order to keep the game short, you can use half a deck (only two suits).
Goal: To get the most cards at the end.
Procedure: Shuffle the cards and deal out all of them, face down. Players simultaneously turn over one card. The player with the largest number gets all the cards.

(3) Review number order

Textbook

Tasks 6-10, pp. 14-15

  7. 10
  8. 5
10. (a) 7; 8; 10
    (b) 6; 4; 3
    (c) 7   0
        2   4
        7   8

Workbook

Exercise 4

  2. (from starting
    position at bottom of
    page)
    3
    10
    8
    7
    0
    5

Teaching activities

Ask your student to make stacks of 1, 2, 3, 4, 5, 6, 7, 8, 9, and 10 multilink cubes, line them up in order, and place numeral cards under them (as in task 6, textbook p. 14).

Ask your student what he can tell you about any pattern he sees. Lead him to see that each number is one more than the one before.

Remove the cubes, and then remove several of the numeral cards and mix the removed cards up. Ask your student to replace them in the correct places.

Repeat these activities, but in reverse order, 10 down to 1. Ask your student to practice counting backwards.

Have your student do tasks 6-10, textbook pp. 14-15.

Reinforcement

Tell your student a number between 1 and 10 and ask her to count on from that number to 10.

Tell your student a number between 1 and 10 and ask him to count down from that number to 1.

Mix up a set of numeral cards 1-10 and ask your student to put them in order, either forward or backward.

Mix up a set of numeral cards 1-10 and remove 4 of them. Place the remaining cards on the table face up and the removed cards face down. Ask your student which cards are missing, without allowing her to move the cards around.

Give your student 3 to 5 random numeral cards (not necessarily consecutive) and ask him to put them in order.

Repeat any of these activities with number word cards.

Unit 2 – Number Bonds

Part 1 – Making Number Stories

Number bonds are different combinations of two numbers that make up a third. In this section, a number bond represents a part-whole relationship between 3 numbers. A number bond is related to a family of four basic addition and subtraction facts. A student can use number bonds to add and subtract. Later, number bonds can be used to show different ways a number can be split up to facilitate mental math or other operations or concepts.

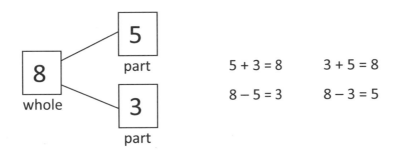

$$5 + 3 = 8 \qquad 3 + 5 = 8$$
$$8 - 5 = 3 \qquad 8 - 3 = 5$$

The part-whole concept is important and will be used throughout *Primary Mathematics* along with number bonds. Later, students will see that if the whole is missing, the two parts must be added to get the missing whole. If a part is missing, the other part must be subtracted from the whole to get the missing part. This concept will help students determine what equation to use later to solve word problems. So this unit is foundational to the rest of the series.

Your student needs to know the number bonds for 1-10. 1 has only one number bond: 1, 1, 0. There are two or more number bonds for each of the rest.

Make sure your student understands that the orientation of the number bonds, drawn with squares here, does not matter. The whole can be on the top, the bottom, the left side, or the right side of the other two parts. Which part goes where does not matter, and whether there are circles or squares around the numbers, or nothing around them, does not matter. What is important is that the drawing distinguishes between the parts and the whole by having lines from the parts to the whole. Thus all of the following are equivalent.

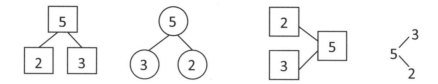

At this stage, it is better to circle or draw squares around the numbers to clearly delineate them from each other.

Spend as much time on this material as needed for your student to commit the number bonds for 1-10 to memory. Don't rush through this unit. Make sure he knows most of the number bonds before moving on. However, if he has a lot of trouble memorizing number bonds, don't stop here long enough to thoroughly bore him; you can continue to have him practice them during the next three units. Some students have an easier time memorizing addition and subtraction facts rather than number bonds, and some helps will be included in the units on addition and subtraction within 10 to help your student memorize those facts.

Students will then learn how to find a missing part of a number bond.

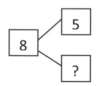

The missing part of a number bond can be visualized in two ways.

1. A set of 8 objects is divided into two parts. One part is 5. What is the other part?

2. Given a set of 5 objects, how many more are needed to make 8?

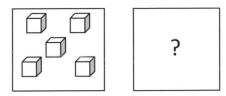

The workbook exercise for this concept includes picture helps. Your student can start out by using objects to find the missing part, but eventually she should be able to do find the missing part without pictures, particularly if she has memorized the number bonds.

Number bonds of 10 are important for later methods of addition and subtraction where the total is greater than 10. Give your student plenty of practice in making ten with activities or games.

Material

Cards with numerals 0-10
Counters
Multilink cubes
Playing cards 0-10
Set of double-nine dominoes (optional)

(1) Understand number bonds; find number bonds for 2, 3, 4, 5, and 6

Textbook

Pages 16-17

Tasks 1-2, p. 18

  1. Answers will vary.
  2. 1, 5; 2, 4; 3, 3

Workbook

Exercise 5

  1. balloons,
     roller skates,
     bow,
     mittens

Teaching activities

Refer to the textbook pp. 16-17. You can use the pictures on these pages, and/or toys that can be grouped in different ways. Ask your student to tell you how many penguins there are and what they are doing. Then ask him to make up number stories for the different pictures. For example:

- There are 5 penguins. 2 are swimming. 3 are outside the water.
- There are 5 penguins. 2 are big. 3 are small.
- There are 5 penguins. 4 are playing. 1 is sleeping.

For each story, point out the number bond. Lead your student to see that one number is the whole, and the other two numbers are parts. The two parts together make the whole. This is indicated by drawing lines from the part to the whole.

Ask your student to make a train of 5 multilink cubes. Then ask her to break it apart into two parts in different ways. List all the possible number bonds. Tell her that 0, 5, and 5 also make a number bond. Be sure she understands that splitting 5 into 1 and 4 is the same as splitting 5 into 4 and 1.

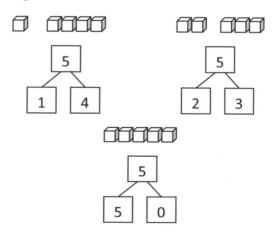

Repeat with 6 multilink cubes.

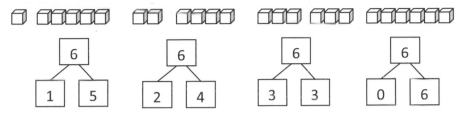

Ask your student to write number bonds for 1, 2, 3, and 4. You can let him use multilink cubes if necessary.

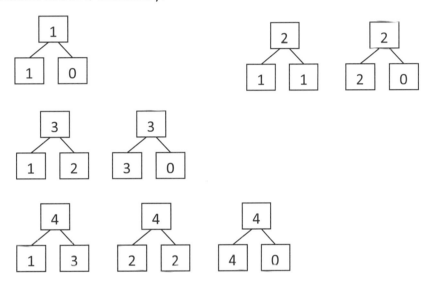

Ask your student to do tasks 1-2, textbook p. 18. Lead him to come up with more than just one story for task 1. Write number bonds for each. For example, there are 2 children in the swing and 4 on the seesaw. There are 3 girls and 3 boys. You can include number bonds with 0; there are 6 children on the swings or seesaw, and 0 just on the grass.

Reinforcement

Use number cards 0-10. Decide on a target number (the whole), such as 5. Set out 5 cards, of which at least two make the target number, such as 2, 3, 4, 6, and 9. Ask your student to pick out the pairs of numbers that make the target number. Repeat with another set of cards, or a different target number.

(2) Find number bonds for 7, 8, 9, and 10

Textbook

Tasks 3-8, pp. 19-21

  3. Answers will vary.
  4. 1, 6; 2, 5; 3, 4; 7, 0
  5. Answers will vary.
  6. 1, 7; 2, 6; 3, 5;
     4, 4; 8, 0
  7. 1, 8; 2, 7; 3, 6;
     4, 5; 9, 0
  8. 1, 9; 2, 8; 3, 7;
     4, 6; 5, 5; 10, 0

Workbook

Exercise 6

  1. 6 , 1; 5, 2; 4,3
     1, 6; 7, 0; 3, 4
     2, 5

Exercise 7

  1. 8 , 0; 7, 1; 4, 4;
     3, 5; HELICOPTER

Exercise 8

  1. 8 , 1; 2, 7; 6, 3;
     7, 2; 4, 5;
     CIRCUS

Exercise 9

  1. 4 ,6; 7, 3; 5, 5;
     0, 10; 9, 1

Teaching activities

Ask your student to use two colors of multilink cubes to make all the number bonds for a particular number (7, 8, 9, or 10), such as 1 red and 7 yellows, 2 reds and 6 yellows, 3 reds and 5 yellows, and 4 reds and 4 yellows for 8. She can continue with the pairs that make the same number bonds but using opposite colors, e.g. 5 reds and 3 yellows, 6 reds and 2 yellows, 7 reds and 1 yellow. Point out that these are the same number bonds as found earlier. Write all the number bonds, and include the ones with 0 as a part. The number bonds for 7, 8, 9, and 10 are given on the next page of this guide.

You may wish to spend one day on number bonds for 7, doing a multilink cube activity and the learning tasks in the textbook, followed by some reinforcement for memorization for number bonds through 7, then the next day on number bonds for 8, and so on. Or, you can introduce all the number bonds in one or two days, and then spend several days with games and other activities to help your student memorize them.

When doing the learning tasks on pages 19-21, get your student to come up with more than just one story. For example, for task 3, there are 6 yellow and 1 green balloon, 3 small and 4 large balloons, 2 without stars and 5 with stars.

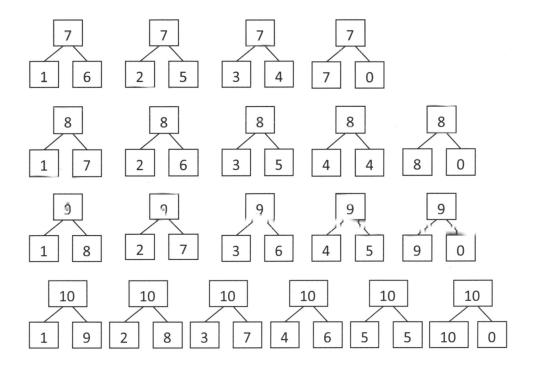

Reinforcement

Use playing cards 1-10. Choose a target number between 6 and 10, which will be the whole. Shuffle the deck and place the whole deck face down. Start by turning over the cards, one at a time, and laying them out in a line in front of your student. As soon as she sees a pair anywhere that makes the target number, she can remove the pair from the line. Fill in the gaps with the next cards turned over. If you want no cards left over, only use cards up to and including the target number.

Game
Material: Playing cards 0-10
Goal: To make pairs of numbers that add up to the target number.
Procedure: Chose a target number, which will be the whole. Use only the cards up and including that number; for example, if the target number is 8, use cards 0-8. Shuffle and put 4 cards out on the table face up and the rest in a pile face down. Players take turns turning over a card from the face-down pile. If the card makes the target number with one of the cards on the table, that player keeps the two cards. Otherwise he leaves it face up on the table.

Enrichment

Use multilink cubes to find number bonds with more than two parts. Ask your student to split the cubes into more than 3 parts, and then write a number bond with more parts. See the first example below.

Write a number, ask your student to tell you two parts that make that whole. Then, for each part greater than 1, continue the process until there are only parts of 1. Ask your student to count the number of 1's at the end; the total 1's should be the same as the number you started with.

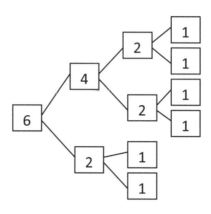

(3) Find the missing part of a number bond

Teaching activities

Set out six to ten counters or other objects. Ask your student how many objects there are.

Cover up some of them and ask him how many are covered up. He can count on his fingers, if that helps, by counting up from the number that is not covered up. Draw the number bond with a blank for the missing part, and fill in the missing part when he has the answer.

Repeat with other amounts.

Draw two circles. In one circle, put 5 objects. Write a number bond with 9 as the whole and 5 as one part.

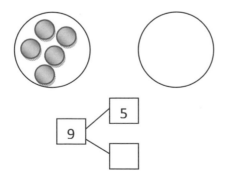

Textbook

Task 9, p. 22

9. (a) 2
   (b) 6   (c) 0
   (d) 2   (e) 3
   (f) 6   (g) 9

Workbook

Exercise 10

2. (a) 2   (b) 2
   (c) 6   (d) 6
3. (a) 3 more
   (b) 2 more
   (c) 3 more
   (d) 4 more

Ask your student to put more objects in the second circle to make 9. Fill in the missing part on the number bond.

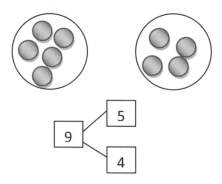

Repeat with other numbers.

Write a number bond with a missing part and ask your student to find the missing part. Allow him to use counters to find the answer, if needed.

Have your student do task 9, textbook p. 22.

Reinforcement

Use playing cards, 0-10. Shuffle. Turn over two cards at a time. The larger number is the whole, and the smaller a part. Ask your student to name the other part.

(4) Practice number bonds that make 10

Teaching activities

Use the dot cards described in the list of manipulatives at the beginning of this guide as "Set 3", i.e. the dot cards for 0-10. Show your student the card for 10. You can leave it out as reference for a while. Mix up the remaining cards and show them to your student, one at a time. Ask him to tell you how many more dots are needed to make 10.

Play the games shown in tasks 10 and 11, textbook p. 23.

Task 10 is a game that can be played by two players. Each player has 10 counters. Players take turns dividing them into two sets, showing one set in an open hand and hiding one set in a fist. The other player must tell the number of objects that are hidden.

For Task 11, you can use playing cards or number cards 0-10. For shorter games or activities use two sets, for longer practice use four sets. There are several ways you can use them.
1. Lay them all out face up, and ask your student to match tens.
2. Shuffle them. Show your student one at a time and ask her to tell you the number needed to make 10 with it.
3. Shuffle and put four cards out on the table face up and the rest in a pile face down. Players take turns turning over a card from the face-down pile. If the card makes 10 with one of the cards on the table, the player keeps the cards. Otherwise he leaves it face up on the table.

Textbook

Tasks 10-11, p. 23

10. 4
11. 0, 10; 1, 9; 2, 8;
    4, 6; 5, 5

Workbook

Exercise 11

1. (a) 3
   (b) 2
2. (a) 6   (b) 1
   (c) 5   (d) 4
3. 5 → 5
   4 → 6
   3 → 7
   2 → 8
   1 → 9
   0 → 10
4. (a) 9   (b) 7
   (c) 4   (d) 8

Reinforcement

Game
Material: Double-nine dominoes
Procedure: Turn the dominoes face down and mix them around. Turn one face up and put it in the center of the playing area. Players take turns taking a domino and matching one end to a domino on the table. The two matched ends must make a 10.

Unit 3 – Addition

Part 1 – Making Addition Stories

In this section, students will learn to write addition equations using the symbols "+" and "=" to represent the mathematical process of finding the total number of objects in two sets. The emphasis is on understanding the meaning of addition, rather than on memorization of facts. Encourage your student to make up addition stories and represent the stories with an addition equation.

The "+" sign means to "put together" and the "=" sign means "is the same as". Read addition equations in a variety of ways to your student, depending on the situation each represents. "5 + 2 = 7" can be read as, "five plus two equals seven" or "five and two is seven" or "5 and 2 more make 7" or "When we put 5 and 2 together, we get 7".

Though the curriculum at this level will write the two parts first, and the total, or whole, last, e.g. 2 + 5 = 7, there is nothing wrong with writing it the other way around: 7 = 2 + 5. The equal sign just means that both sides evaluate to the same number and does not dictate that what comes after it has to be the "answer" to the addition problem. This is an important concept that most students are not exposed to until later. You might want to write some of the equations with the total first to get your student used to seeing it that way. In general, though, as we think through a problem, we write the calculations we must do first, "2 + 5", and then find the answer and write it.

There are three addition situations illustrated on p. 24.
1. Putting together: Put together 3 butterflies and 4 butterflies. There are 7 butterflies altogether.
2. Part-whole: The 6 red flowers and 4 yellow flowers are two parts of a whole. 10 is the whole. 6 and 4 make 10.
3. Adding on: Add 2 more children to the 3 children already in the sandbox. There will be 5 children altogether.

Illustrate three different addition situations using objects. In the teaching activities below, counters are used, but you can use other objects.

Material

Counters, other objects for addition stories: toys, pictures, etc.

(1) Understand the meaning of addition

Textbook
Page 24

Workbook

Exercise 12

1. (a) 3; 4; 7
   (b) 4; 4; 8
   (c) 2; 4; 6
2. (a) 5
   (b) 9
   (c) 10
   (d) 7

Exercise 13

1. (a) 2; 5
   (b) 1; 9
   (c) 3; 7
   (d) 4; 9

Teaching activities

Illustrate the three addition situations using counters or other objects. The names for the different situations are for your benefit; do not name them for your student. Make up stories to go along with the situations.

Part-whole:

Show 3 counters of one color and 6 of another. Ask your student for the number in each group, and then ask how many there are altogether. For example, there are 3 cardinals in the yard and 6 blue-jays. How many birds are there in the yard?

Putting together:

Show 5 objects in one group, and 2 in another group. Ask your student to count the number in each group. Then put them together into a single group. Ask him to tell you the total number. Say, "Putting 5 and 2 together make 7."

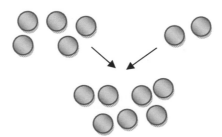

Adding on:

Draw a circle and put 4 counters in it, and 2 counters outside of it. Make up a story, such as; there are 4 frogs in the pond, and two on the bank. The two on the bank jump in the pond. Ask your student how many are in the pond. Move the counters from outside the circle into it, while she counts on from 4 to the total of 6. Say: 4 and 2 more make 6.

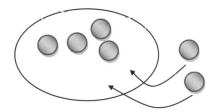

Discuss page 24 in the textbook. Ask your student to count the red flowers and the yellow flowers, and then tell you how many flowers there are altogether. Then ask him to count the butterflies on the flowers, and the ones not on the flowers, and then tell you how many butterflies there are altogether. Ask him to count the children in the sandbox and the children coming to the sandbox, and then tell you how many children there are altogether.

Reinforcement

Use toys, pictures, or real-life situations to give your student more practice in creating addition stories.

(2) Relate addition stories to an addition equation

Textbook

Pages 25-26

Tasks 1-3, pp. 27-29

Answers will vary.

Workbook

Exercise 14

1. (a) 8 + 1
   (b) 3 + 5
   (c) 6 + 1
   (d) 7 + 3
2. (a) 5 + 3; 3 + 5
   (b) 5 + 1; 4 + 2; 3 + 3
3. (a) 3 + 2 = 5
   (b) 3 + 3 = 6
   (c) 2 + 5 = 7
   (d) 5 + 4 = 9

Teaching activities

Show your student 2 groups of the same objects, such as 7 counters in one group, and 2 in another group. Ask your student how many there are in each group.

Then move them together into one group and ask your student how many there are altogether. Tell her that we can show what is happening by writing an equation. Write: 7 + 2 = 9.

　　　7 + 2 = 9

Point to each part of the equation as you read it: 7 plus 2 equals 9.

Tell your student that "+" is called a plus sign. It means we are putting together the numbers on each side of it. The "=" means "is the same as" or "equals". The "7 + 2" on one side of the "=" sign is the same as "9" on the other side. Tell him we call a number sentence with an equal sign an **equation**. This type of number equation is an addition equation.

Tell your student that 7 + 2 = 9 is a true statement, so it is a *fact*. When she sees an expression such as 7 + 2, and then gives the answer, she is giving an addition fact.

Show your student 2 sets of different objects, such as 4 counters of one color and 3 of another, or 4 multilink cubes and 3 counters. Ask him for the number in each group, and for the total. Say: 4 and 3 make 7.

Tell your student that since we are finding the total, we can also show what is happening by writing an addition equation. Write: 4 + 3 = 7.

4 + 3 = 7

Read the equation: 4 plus 3 equals 7.

Draw a circle and put 7 counters in it, and 3 counters outside of it. Ask your student how many are in the circle. Have your student count on as you add the 3 to the circle. Say: 7 and 3 more make 10. Tell her we also use the plus sign and write an addition equation to show that the first number is joined by more to make the total amount. Write: 7 + 3 = 10.

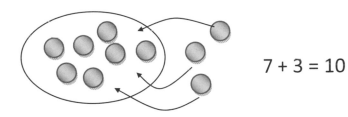

7 + 3 = 10

Repeat with other examples, asking your student to write the addition equation.

Discuss textbook pp. 25-26. Ask your student to do tasks 1-3, textbook pp. 27-29.

Reinforcement

Use toys, pictures, or real-life situations to give your student more practice in making number stories and writing addition equations. Try to find instances of each of the three types of addition situations.

Part 2 – Addition with Number Bonds

The number bonds learned in unit 2 will help your student master both the addition and subtraction facts within 10. These facts are associated with the part-whole concept of number bonds. Given a number bond we can write two related addition facts and two related subtraction facts.

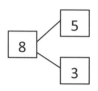

$$5 + 3 = 8 \qquad 3 + 5 = 8$$
$$8 - 5 = 3 \qquad 8 - 3 = 5$$

Help your student commit the addition facts to memory. Some students can memorize these number facts easily with only a little drill; others may need additional help through games and structured activities. Some students, even those who excel at math comprehension, will always have trouble memorizing math facts, though they will probably be able to memorize the facts through 10 easily enough. Strategies for computing the facts through 20 from the facts through 10 will be given in a later unit.

At this stage, most students already know addition facts within 5 and some easier addition facts such as +1.

0 + 0	0 + 1	0 + 2	0 + 3	0 + 4	0 + 5	0 + 6	0 + 7	0 + 8	0 + 9	0 + 10
1 + 0	1 + 1	1 + 2	1 + 3	1 + 4	1 + 5	1 + 6	1 + 7	1 + 8	1 + 9	
2 + 0	2 + 1	2 + 2	2 + 3							
3 + 0	3 + 1	3 + 2								
4 + 0	4 + 1									
5 + 0	5 + 1									
6 + 0	6 + 1									
7 + 0	7 + 1									
8 + 0	8 + 1									
9 + 0	9 + 1									
10 + 0										

After this section, help your student memorize these facts, and then add new facts as you go through succeeding lessons and units.

Use flash cards, computer games where you can set the facts that are to be practiced, etc. Since first graders are still working on fine-motor skills, using worksheets, particularly timed ones, may not be a good idea, unless they are done orally. There are many web sites that will print out drill sheets to specification; you can use them and ask your student to look at the problem and answer orally if writing is an issue.

There are mental math worksheets in the appendix you can copy and use.

Material

Counters
Other objects for addition stories: toys, pictures, etc.
Fact game cards for addition facts within 5, +0, and +1

(1) Add within ten by recalling the related number bond

Textbook

Page 30

Tasks 1-2, p. 31

1. 8
2. 7

Workbook

Exercise 15

1. (a) 8; 8, 6, 2
   (b) 6; 6, 1, 5
   (c) 10; 10, 3, 7
   (d) 5; 5, 2, 3
2. 9   7
   6   8
   9   10
3. 6: 4 + 2; 3 + 3; 2 + 4
   8: 3 + 5; 4 + 4; 5 + 3
   5: 5 + 0; 1 + 4; 3 + 2
   7: 0 + 7; 4 + 3; 6 + 1
   9: 6 + 3; 5 + 4; 2 + 7

Exercise 16

1. 8; 8
2. 9; 9
3. 8; 8
4. 8; 8

Teaching activities

Show your student 2 sets of different objects, such as 4 counters of one color and 3 of another, or 4 multilink cubes and 3 counters, or two sets of similar toys. Ask her to write the addition equation.

$$3 + 4 = 7$$

Tell your student that we have two parts and are finding the whole. So we can draw a number bond for this situation. One part plus the other part equals the whole.

$$3 + 4 = 7$$

Write a number bond. Ask your student to tell you an addition number story to go along with the number bond. Provide objects for props if that appeals to your student. Write two addition equations for the number bond.

$$6 + 4 = 10$$
$$4 + 6 = 10$$

Repeat with another number bond. This time ask your student to write the two addition equations.

Discuss textbook p. 30. Have your student do tasks 1-2, textbook p. 31.

(2) Add within ten using number bonds

Teaching activities

Have your student do task 3, textbook p. 32. Ask him to make up an addition story for the two situations.

Tell your student an addition story involving a sum within 10. Draw a number bond and help her fill it in with the information in the story, and find the total. If she has memorized the number bonds, she should be able to find the total without needing objects, but if she has not, allow her to work out the answer with counters.

Repeat with other stories. Try to use each of the addition situations – part-whole, putting together, and adding on.

Reinforcement

Game
Material: Flash cards for addition facts through 5, +0, and +1 with answers on separate cards.
Procedure: Mix up the cards and put them all face down. Turn over the first card and put it in the middle. Players take turns turning over cards. If a card matches one that is face up, i.e. it is the answer to a fact or a fact for an answer, the player gets to keep both cards. Otherwise, he puts the card he turned over face up on the table.

Mental Math 1

Textbook

Task 3, p.32

3. (a) 6   (b) 10

Workbook

Exercise 17

1. (a) 7   (b) 7
   (c) 4   (d) 7
2. 9; 9
3. 10; 10

Part 3 – Other Methods of Addition

This section introduces students to the "count on" strategy. This strategy will help students work out harder addition facts before they can memorize them. Your student can use this strategy for +2 and +3 addition facts, and, if she knows doubles, with doubles + 1 facts (e.g., 3 + 4, 4 + 5).

Your student will probably be able to count up 1, 2, or 3 without using fingers. Fingers can be used if needed to begin with. Counting up for larger numbers is not taught since it becomes harder to keep track of how many are added on and to know where to stop without fingers or number lines. Also, adding numbers where the sum is larger than 10 is taught in the context of the base-10 concept of our number system in Unit 6, rather than simply adding more numbers on. It is important that students think of numbers in the context of tens and ones, not just one more.

When your student does count up, be sure he is not including the number that he is counting on from. For example, for 6 + 3 a student might say 6, 7, 8, and stop there, since he has counted up 3 numbers. Teach him to "think" 6, and then count up 3 from there: 7, 8, 9.

Extra time is spent in this section on pairs of numbers that "make 10". If your student has learned the number bonds to 10, she might know the addition facts for 10 already.

The only addition facts within 10 not included in sums to 5, +1, +2, +3, and "make 10" are 4 + 4, 4 + 5, and 5 + 4. Teach your student doubles (1 + 1, 2 + 2, 3 + 3, 4 + 4, 5 + 5). Then, 4 + 5, 5 + 4, as well as 3 + 4 and 4 + 3, are doubles + 1.

Dot cards (see the section on manipulatives) can help students visualize the addition facts for adding on to 5, the facts that make 10, doubles (e.g. 4 + 4), and doubles + 1 (e.g. 4 + 5 is the same as double 4 + one more). Students should be able to recognize numbers from dot patterns without having to count.

Continue with helping your student commit the addition facts to memory using games, drills, etc. After finishing this section, add the rest of the addition facts through 10 to those listed on p. 24 of this guide:

0 + 0   0 + 1   0 + 2   0 + 3   0 + 4   0 + 5   0 + 6   0 + 7   0 + 8   0 + 9   0 + 10
1 + 0   1 + 1   1 + 2   1 + 3   1 + 4   1 + 5   1 + 6   1 + 7   1 + 8   1 + 9
2 + 0   2 + 1   2 + 2   2 + 3   **2 + 4**   **2 + 5**   **2 + 6**   **2 + 7**   **2 + 8**
3 + 0   3 + 1   3 + 2   **3 + 3**   **3 + 4**   **3 + 5**   **3 + 6**   **3 + 7**
4 + 0   4 + 1   **4 + 2**   **4 + 3**   **4 + 4**   **4 + 5**   **4 + 6**
5 + 0   5 + 1   **5 + 2**   **5 + 3**   **5 + 4**   **5 + 5**
6 + 0   6 + 1   **6 + 2**   **6 + 3**   **6 + 4**
7 + 0   7 + 1   **7 + 2**   **7 + 3**
8 + 0   8 + 1   **8 + 2**
9 + 0   9 + 1
10 + 0

Material

Counters
Fact cards for addition through 10, with answers on separate cards
Number cube labeled +1 on two sides, +2 on two sides, and +3 on two sides
Number cards (or playing cards) 0-10, 4 sets
Dot cards for "Making 10", doubles, doubles + 1

(1) Count on to add 1, 2, or 3 to a number within 10

Textbook

Page 33

4 + 1 = 5
4 + 2 = 6
4 + 3 = 7

Tasks 1-4, pp. 34-35

1. 6 + 1 = 7
2. 7 + 2 = 9
3. 4 + 3 = 77
4. (a) 4   (b) 6
        5   8
        8   10
   (c) 5   (d) 8
        8   9
        10   10

Workbook

Exercise 18

1. (a) 5   (b) 9
   (c) 6   (d) 10
2. 7; 4; 5
3. 10; 7; 9
4. 6; 9; 10

Teaching activities

Draw a number line for 0-10, or lay out number cards 1 to 10 in order. Write the expression: 5 + 1. Tell your student to put his finger on the number 5. Then tell him to hop forward 1 space, counting up as he does so: 6. Write the answer to the expression. Now write the expression: 5 + 2. Ask him to find the answer using the number line. Repeat with 5 + 3. Repeat with other addition problems within 10.

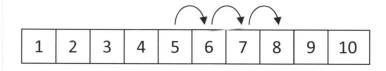

| 1 | 2 | 3 | 4 | 5 | 6 | 7 | 8 | 9 | 10 |

5 + 3 = 8

Write the expression: 6 + 3. Write the numeral 6 and then write 3 dots, or use 3 counters. Ask your student to supply the answer by using the dots or counters to count on from 6. Then write the expression: 3 + 6. Ask her to find the answer. Lead her to see that she can find the answer in the same way as with 6 + 3, not by counting up from 3. Repeat with other addition problems within 10, adding 1, 2, or 3.

6 + 3 | 6 | ●●●   6 + 3 = 9
                    ●   3 + 6 = 9

Discuss textbook p. 33. Your student should start with 4, and then count on to add the frogs on the second lily pad.

Have your student do tasks 1-4, textbook pp. 34-35.

Reinforcement

Game
Material: Number line 0-10, with squares large enough for counters, counters, number cube labeled +1 on two sides, +2 on two sides, and +3 on two sides.
Procedure: Each player puts his or her counter at the beginning of the number line. Players take turns throwing the number cube and moving their counter on the number line by the amount face-up on the cube. If one player lands on another player's position, the other player goes back to 0. If the player is near 10 and the amount on the number cube causes the player to go past 10, the player goes back to 0. The first player to land on 10 wins.

Mental Math 2-3

(2) Learn addition facts for 10, doubles + 1

Textbook

Tasks 5-6, pp. 36-37

5. (a) 9   (b) 8
  (c) 7   (d) 6
  (e) 5   (f) 4
  (g) 3   (h) 2
  (i) 1   (j) 0

6. 10: 8 + 2, 4 + 6,
     3 + 7. 7 + 3,
     2 + 8, 9 + 1,
     5 + 5, 6 + 4
  9: 4 + 5, 7 + 2,
     6 + 3, 3 + 6,
     2 + 7, 0 + 9,
     5 + 4, 8 + 1

Workbook

Exercise 19

1. turtle

Teaching activities

Use counters or other small objects. Set out 6 of them in two rows. Write the expression: 3 + 3. Ask your student to find the answer. Then add another disk to one row. Write the expression: 3 + 4. Lead your student to see that he can find the answer from the answer to 3 + 3 by counting on 1.

        3 + 3 = 6   3 + 4 = 7

Ask for the answer to 2 + 2, and then 2 + 3, by saying 2 + 3 is one more than 2 + 2.

Ask for the answer to 4 + 4, and then 4 + 5, by saying 4 + 5 is one more than 4 + 4. Illustrate with discs if necessary.

Give your student the dot cards for making 10 and ask her to write two addition equations for each. For example:

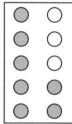   7 + 3 = 10
                     3 + 7 = 10

Have your student do tasks 5-6, textbook pp. 36-37.

Reinforcement

Games

<u>Material</u>: Number 0-10, 4 sets (or playing cards).
<u>Procedure</u>: Shuffle the cards and place them face down. Players take turns turning over two cards. If the two cards make a ten, they keep the cards; otherwise the cards go into a discard pile. When the cards are used up, the discard pile is shuffled and turned face down and the game resumes until all cards are used. The winner has the most cards.

<u>Material</u>: Flash cards for addition facts through 10 and answers on separate cards.
<u>Procedure</u>: Mix up the cards and put them all face down. Turn over the first card and put it in the middle. Players take turns turning over cards. If a card matches one that is face up, i.e. it is the answer to a fact or a fact for an answer, the player gets to keep both cards. Otherwise, he puts the card he turned over face up on the table.

Mental Math 4-5

Unit 4 – Subtraction

Part 1 – Making Subtraction Stories

Subtraction is the reverse process of addition. Instead of adding on, we take away. When two parts or sets are put together, we add to find how many there are altogether. If one part is missing, we subtract to find out how many are in the missing part.

The "–" (minus) sign means to "take away". Read subtraction equations in a variety of ways to your student, depending on the situation they represent. For example, "8 – 3 = 5" can be read as, "eight take away three is five" or "eight minus three equals five" or "When we subtract three from eight, we get five".

In this part, the emphasis is on understanding the meaning of subtraction, rather than the memorization of facts. Encourage your child to make up stories to illustrate subtraction.

There are two subtraction situations on p. 38.

1. Taking away: Take 3 carrots from 9; there are 6 carrots left. 8 birds are on a branch, three fly away (take away 3), there are 5 left.
2. Part-whole: There are 7 children. 2 are girls. How many are boys? Subtract to find out.

Another subtraction situation – finding the difference between two sets – will be taught in the first unit of *Primary Mathematics 1B*.

Illustrate subtraction concretely. In the teaching activities below, counters are used, but you can use other objects.

Material

Counters, pennies
Other objects for subtraction stories: toys, pictures, etc.

(1) Understand the meaning of subtraction

Teaching activities

Illustrate some subtraction situations.

Find the part left:
Show 7 objects in a group together. Make up a story about them, e.g. there are 7 cars.

Cover them up with an index card, or put something in front of them so your student does not see them. Move two objects out so he can see them. Tell your student that 2 went away, e.g., 2 cars drove off. Ask how many are left. After he answers, show how many are left.

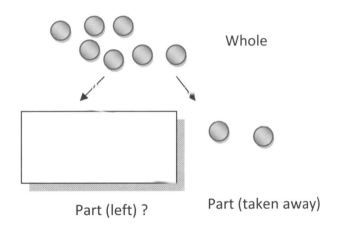

Whole

Part (left) ?   Part (taken away)

Find the missing part:
Show 5 objects in a group together. Use objects that are different on one side than the other, such as pennies or counters with a mark on one side. Then hide them from view and turn 2of them over. Show the 2 you have turned over. Tell your student that you have 5 pennies, 2 of them have the tails facing up. Ask her how many have tails facing down (and heads up). After she answers, show the hidden ones. (See next page.)

Textbook

Page 38

Workbook

Exercise 20

1. (a) 2; 3 (b) 2; 4
   (c) 1; 6 (d) 4; 5
2. (a) 3   (b) 3
   (c) 6   (d) 7

Exercise 21

1. (a) 2   (b) 4
   (c) 3   (d) 3
2. (a) 4   (b) 5
   (c) 4   (d) 2

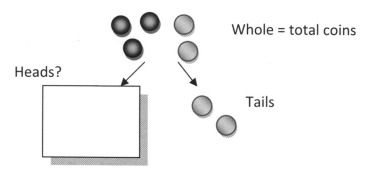

Find the part taken away:

Show 6 objects in a group together. Make up a story about them, e.g. there are 6 dogs. Again hide them from your student in some way, and take some away. This time keep the part taken away hidden and show the part left. Tell your student that some went away (e.g., some dogs went away and 4 did not) and ask how many went away. After your student answers, show how many went away.

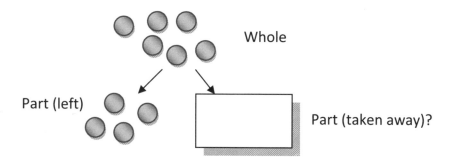

Discuss p. 38 in the textbook. Ask your student to make up stories involving finding a part. For example, there were 8 birds on the branch. Three flew away. How many are left? Or, some flew away, and 5 stayed. How many flew away? There were 9 carrots. The bunnies ate 3 of them. How many are left? There are 7 children. 2 are girls. How many boys are there?

(1) Relate subtraction stories to subtraction equations

Teaching activities

Make up a subtraction story, e.g. there are 9 balloons. Three of them popped. How many are left? Illustrate with counters or other objects. Tell your student we can show what is happening by writing an equation. Write: $9 - 3 = 6$.

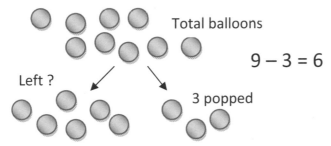

Point to each part of the equation as you read it: 9 take away 3 is 6.

Tell your student that "–" is called a minus sign and means we are taking away one part. The equal sign means that both sides mean the same thing, or are equal to each other. An equation with a minus sign and an equal sign is called a subtraction equation.

Repeat with other examples, similar to the examples in the previous lesson, asking your student to write the equation.

Discuss pages 39-40 in the textbook, and have your student do tasks 1-3, textbook pp. 41-43.

Reinforcement

Use toys, pictures, or real-life situations to give your student more practice in making number stories and writing subtraction equations.

Textbook

Pages 39-40

Tasks 1-3, pp. 41-43

Answers will vary.

Workbook

Exercise 22

1. (a) $6 - 2$ (b) $6 - 2$
   (c) $4 - 1$ (d) $7 - 2$
2. (a) $6 - 4$; $6 - 1$
   (b) $7 - 6$; $7 - 3$
3. (a) $6 - 2 = 4$; $6 - 4 = 2$
   (b) $7 - 3 = 4$; $7 - 4 = 3$
   (c) $5 - 2 = 3$; $5 - 3 = 2$
   (d) $8 - 3 = 5$; $8 - 5 = 3$

Part 2 – Methods of Subtraction

As with addition facts, subtraction facts are associated with the part-whole concept of number bonds. Given a number bond we can write two related addition equations and two related subtraction equation.

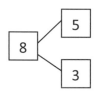

$$5 + 3 = 8 \qquad 3 + 5 = 8$$
$$8 - 5 = 3 \qquad 8 - 3 = 5$$

As the student learned in the previous lesson, we write an addition equation to show that, given the parts, we are finding the whole:

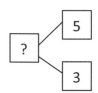

$$5 + 3 = 8 \qquad 3 + 5 = 8$$

If we are given the whole, or total amount, and one part, we use a subtraction equation to show that we are finding a missing part.

 $8 - 3 = 5$ 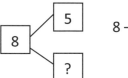 $8 - 5 = 3$

In this section, your student will write a family of four related addition and subtraction facts. She needs to realize that we use an addition equation to put two parts together, so the answer will be larger than each part. We use a subtraction equation to show that we start with a whole, or total, and know one part, but need to find a missing part. The missing part can either be the part taken away, or the part left. The answer to a subtraction equation is always smaller than the whole, and we subtract from the larger number. This concept is reinforced in the exercises in which the student has to insert the missing operand ('+' or '–").

Counting back can help students work out the subtraction facts for subtracting 1, 2, and 3 before they memorize them. Counting back 1, 2, 3 is doable without manipulatives, but counting back larger numbers than 3 usually needs some way to keep track of how many numbers have been counted back, such as fingers or a number line. Since counting back is meant to help students calculate mentally, the "count back" strategy is restricted to 1, 2, or 3.

When counting back, make sure your student does not make the common error of including the number that is being counted back from. He needs to begin with that number, but count back from there. Introducing the strategy with a number line can help your student not make this error, since he counts the number of hops.

Another strategy students can use to find the answer to a subtraction equation is to recognize when two numbers are 1, 2, or 3 apart. If the numbers are not too far apart, it is easy to count up from the part to the whole to find the answer. For example, in 8 – 6, start at 6, count up 2 to get to 8, so 8 – 6 = 2. Task 9 in the textbook includes numbers that are 1 or 2 apart, but this strategy can be used for numbers that are 3 apart as well, as most students can keep track of counting up 3 without manipulatives.

Students should be thoroughly familiar with pairs of numbers that make 10 by now, and so be able to answer problems where a number is subtracted from 10. For students who make pictures in their minds, visualizing the 5 by 2 dot pattern on a dot card can be useful in helping them with subtraction from 10.

Help your student commit the subtraction facts to memory. After lesson 1, begin with facts within 5, which your student should be able to master quickly by recalling number bonds. After lesson 3, you can include subtracting 1, 2, or 3 from numbers within 10. After lesson 4, include numbers that differ by 1, 2, or 3, and the rest of the subtraction facts for 10. You can work with these facts a little each day as you continue with the lessons in the textbook. If your student has trouble, you can divide the facts up into the following groups and work with specific groups before combining.

Subtract equal numbers:

$0-0$ $1-1$ $2-2$ $3-3$ $4-4$ $5-5$ $6-6$ $7-7$ $8-8$ $9-9$ $10-10$

Subtract 0:

$0-0$ $1-0$ $2-0$ $3-0$ $4-0$ $5-0$ $6-0$ $7-0$ $8-0$ $9-0$ $10-0$

Subtract 1:

$1-1$ $2-1$ $3-1$ $4-1$ $5-1$ $6-1$ $7-1$ $8-1$ $9-1$ $10-1$

Subtract 2:

$2-2$ $3-2$ $4-2$ $5-2$ $6-2$ $7-2$ $8-2$ $9-2$ $10-2$

Subtract 3:

$3-3$ $4-3$ $5-3$ $6-3$ $7-3$ $8-3$ $9-3$ $10-3$

Subtract a number that is one less:

$1-0$ $2-1$ $3-2$ $4-3$ $5-4$ $6-5$ $7-6$ $8-7$ $9-8$ $10-9$

Subtract a number that is two less:

$2-0$ $3-1$ $4-2$ $5-3$ $6-4$ $7-5$ $8-6$ $9-7$ $10-8$

Subtract a number that is three less:

$4-1$ $5-2$ $6-3$ $7-4$ $8-5$ $9-6$ $10-7$

Remaining facts:

$8-4$ $9-4$ $9-5$ $10-4$ $10-5$ $10-6$

Use computer games where specific facts can be set, or play variation of the suggested games in the previous section. Use activities or games where the student sees the fact in the form of an expression with the minus sign, rather than the type of games suggested in the number bond section, unless your student still needs practice with number bonds. By now, the student should be learning to look at the abstract expression, even if he is thinking pictures in his head to help find the answer. Eventually mix in both addition and subtraction facts.

In lesson 6, your student will learn how to determine whether the answer to a math story requires addition or subtraction. This can be a challenge for many students. At this stage, most of the story is in the form of a picture. Do not try to get your student to rely on key words. Study the problems in Exercises 30 and 31. In Exercise 31 the word altogether is found in the stories that require addition, but in Exercise 21, problem 2 uses the word altogether in a subtraction story. The stories do not deliberately use words like "left" or "taken away" to cue the student to a subtraction equation.

In helping your student determine whether to add or subtract, ask leading questions to get her to think in terms of part and whole, or total. Does the story give two parts and ask for a total amount? Does the story give a total amount, and a part, and ask for another part?

The pictures will help the student in the workbook exercise, but in later exercises, the student will not have a picture. Encourage your student to act out the story, or to use counters to represent the story, or to draw a picture, if he is having difficulty deciding whether to add or subtract.

In some stories, your student might want to write an equation in the form $3 + ? = 7$, where ? is the number that is the answer to the question posed by the story, rather than a subtraction equation. This is a legitimate equation, but during teaching time ask your student to also write a subtraction equation. Your student needs to be able to write subtraction equations. Later in this curriculum, an equation such as $312 +$ ____ $= 432$ is solved with subtraction: ____ $= 432 - 312$, and in algebra, when showing the steps for the solution, subtraction is used: $312 + n = 432$; $n = 432 - 312$.

Material

Counters
Other objects for addition stories: toys, pictures, etc.
Fact game cards for subtraction facts within 10
Number cards 0-10, cards with "+", "–", "="
Number cube labeled –1 on two sides, –2 on two sides, and –3 on two sides.

(1) Subtract within ten by recalling the related number bond

Textbook

p. 44

Tasks 1-3, pp. 45-46

1. 4
2. 3
3. (a) 6   (b) 3

Workbook

Exercise 23

1. 3; 2; 3
   3; 4; 1; 3
   0; 6; 0; 6
   2; 9; 2; 7
2. 4   3
   6   3
   7   6

Exercise 24

1. 5; 5
2. 2; 2
3. 5; 5
4. 6; 6

Teaching activities

Set out 8 counters. Make up a story, such as: "There are 8 cookies. We set 5 aside to eat later." Move 5 away from the 8. Ask your student how many are left. Draw a number bond to represent this, writing 8 and saying that this is the total number of cookies, then 5 and saying that this is the number we set aside. Then write a question mark in the other part of the number bond. Tell your student this is what we want to find, the missing part of the number bond. Tell her that we use the minus sign to show that we want to find a missing part. Write both an addition and subtraction equations with a question mark for the missing part. Then write the subtraction equation with the answer.

$$8 + ? = 5$$
$$8 - 5 = ?$$
$$8 - 5 = 3$$

Draw some number bonds with a missing part and ask your student to write the subtraction equation and the answer.

$$7 - 4 = 3$$

Discuss textbook p. 44 and have your student do tasks 1-3, textbook pp. 45-56. You can ask your student to make up stories for task 3.

(2) Write a family of addition and subtraction equations

Teaching activities

Show your student two sets of related items, such as toy cars and airplanes, or two colors of counters. Make up a story for an addition equation, such as, "Toby has 3 cars and 4 planes. How many toys does he have altogether?" Ask your student to write two addition equations. Then make up a story such as "Toby has 7 cars and planes. 3 of them are cars. How many are planes?" Ask your student to write the subtraction equation. Repeat with the related situation, e.g., "Toby has 7 toy cars and planes. He put all his 4 planes away. How many cars does he have out still?" Point out that there are now four equations, two for addition and two for subtraction.

$$3 + 4 = 7$$
$$4 + 3 = 7$$
$$7 - 3 = 4$$
$$7 - 4 = 3$$

Write an addition or subtraction equation. Ask your student to draw a number bond for it, and then write the other three related addition or subtraction equations.

Textbook

Task 4, p. 47

4. (a) $3 + 2 = 5$ $5 - 2 = 3$
      $2 + 3 = 5$ $5 - 3 = 2$
   (b) $7 + 2 = 9$ $9 - 2 = 7$
      $2 + 7 = 9$ $9 - 7 = 2$

Workbook

Exercise 25

1. (a) 6; 6; 1; 5
   (b) 7; 7; 3; 4
   (c) 5; 5; 3; 2
2. (a) $5 + 2 = 7$ $2 + 5 = 7$
      $7 - 2 = 5$ $7 - 5 = 2$
   (b) $6 + 4 = 10$ $4 + 6 = 10$
      $10 - 6 = 4$ $10 - 4 = 6$
   (c) $6 + 3 = 9$ $3 + 6 = 9$
      $9 - 3 = 6$ $9 - 6 = 3$

Exercise 26

1. $-$ $-$
   $+$ $-$
   $-$ $+$
2. $10 - 3 = 7$ or $10 - 7 = 3$
   $3 + 4 = 7$ or $4 + 3 = 7$
   $6 + 0 = 6$ or $0 + 6 = 6$
   $9 - 2 = 7$ or $9 - 7 = 2$
   $8 - 5 = 3$ or $8 - 3 = 5$

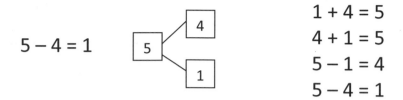

$$5 - 4 = 1$$

$$1 + 4 = 5$$
$$4 + 1 = 5$$
$$5 - 1 = 4$$
$$5 - 4 = 1$$

Have your student do task 4, textbook p. 47.

Set out three number cards that belong in a number bond, and two sign cards, an "=" sign and either "+" or "–". Ask your student to arrange them in an equation. Repeat with other cards.

Reinforcement

Set out six number cards for two different number bonds, two "=" cards, a "+" card, and a "–" card and ask your student to use the cards to make up two number equations. Repeat, this time with the cards needed to make three number equations.

Mental Math 6

(3) Count back to subtract 1, 2, or 3 from a number within 10

Teaching activities

Draw a number line for 0 to10, or lay out number cards 1 to 10 in order. Write the expression 8 – 1. Tell your student to put her finger on the number 8. Then tell her to hop backwards 1 space, counting down as she does so: 7. The answer to 8 – 1 is 7. Write the answer to the expression. Now write the expression 8 – 2 and ask her to hop backwards two spaces from 8 and tell you the answer. Then repeat with 8 – 3. Repeat with other subtraction problems within 10.

1	2	3	4	5	6	7	8	9	10

$$8 - 3 = 5$$

Write an expression such as: 7 – 3. Draw a circle and put 7 counters in it. Ask your student to count them, and then move one counter aside, saying "6", and continue until 3 counters are set aside. Point out that the number he says last is the answer to 7 – 3. Repeat with other subtraction problems within 10, subtracting 1, 2, or 3.

$$7 - 3 = 4$$

Have your student do tasks 5-8, textbook pp. 48-49.

Textbook

Tasks 5-8, pp. 48-49

5. 4
6. 5
7. 7
8. (a) 3   (b) 3
        5   6
        8   8
    (c) 3   (d) 2
        4   5
        8   6

Workbook

Exercise 27

1. (a) 4   (b) 5
   (c) 6   (d) 7
2. 5; 3; 7
3. 5; 3; 7
4. 2; 5; 7

Reinforcement

Game

<u>Material</u>: Number line 0-10, with squares large enough for counters, counters, number cube labeled "−1" on two sides, "−2" on two sides, and "−3" on two sides.

<u>Procedure:</u> Each player puts his or her counter at the end of the number line on 10. Players take turns throwing the number cube and moving their counter. If one player lands on another player's position, the other player goes back to 10. If the player is near 0 and the amount on the number cube causes the player to go past 0, the player goes back to 10. The first player to land on 0 wins.

Mental Math 7

(4) Recognize numbers that differ by 1 or 2, subtract from 10

Teaching activities

Draw a number strip of 10 squares labeled with the numbers 1 to10, or lay out number cards 1 to 10 in order. Write the expression: 8 – 6. Ask your student to locate the two numbers on the number line. Point out that these numbers are close to each other. Ask her to find out how close by counting up from 6 to 8. Write: 8 – 6 = 2. Tell your student than when two numbers are close to each other in a subtraction equation; it is easy to find the answer by counting on from the smaller number to the larger number.

1	2	3	4	5	6	7	8	9	10

$$8 - 6 = 2$$

Repeat with numbers that are 1, 2, or 3 apart, writing the subtraction expression and having your student count up to find the answer.

Give your student the dot cards for making 10 and ask him to write two subtraction equations for each. For example:

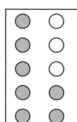

$$10 - 7 = 3$$
$$10 - 3 = 7$$

Have your student do tasks 9-11, textbook p. 50.

Textbook

Task 9-11, p. 50

9. (a) 0   (b) 0
     1   1
     2   2
   (c) 1   (d) 2
     1   2
     1   3
10. 4
11. (a) 7   (b) 5
   (c) 2   (d) 1

Workbook

Exercise 28

1. mountain, houses, field, sky and river

Reinforcement

Game
Material: Flash cards for subtraction facts through 10 and answers on separate cards.
Procedure: Mix up the cards and put them all face down. Turn over the first card and put it in the middle. Players take turns turning over cards. If a card matches one that is face up, i.e. it is the answer to a fact or a fact for an answer, the player gets to keep both cards. Otherwise, he puts the card he turned over face up on the table.

Mental Math 8-9

(5) Review addition and subtraction facts

Teaching activities

Use drill sheets, fact cards, or games to practice the addition and subtraction facts through 10. You can use the mental math pages at the back of this guide. You can give your student the same sheet each day, and use a timer to see how far he gets in 3 minutes. If your student has trouble writing, do them orally. You can also see how many fact cards he can get correct in 3 minutes. Fact cards can be mixed up each time, or you can select only the facts that are causing difficulty.

Reinforcement

Use playing cards 1-10, or 4 sets of number cards 1-10, and 4 cards each with "+", "−", and "=". If you have old decks of cards, you can use the face cards and put some masking tape on them marked with the plus, minus, or equal sign. Shuffle the cards, turn the deck face down, and ask your student to draw one card at a time and lay them out on the table face up. Every time she lays one down, she should look over the cards to see if she can spot a set of 3 numeral cards, a plus or minus card, and an equal card that will make an addition or subtraction equation. If so, she can remove them.

Game
Material: Playing cards 1-10, or 4 sets of number cards 1-10, and 4 cards each with "+", "−", and "=".
Procedure: Shuffle the cards and place them face down. Players take turns drawing cards one at a time and seeing if they can form an addition or subtraction equation with the cards drawn. If so, the player should set the cards down showing the equation. The goal is to end of with the fewest cards still in hand.

Mental Math 10

Textbook

Task 12, p. 51

12. train 5: $9 - 4$;
$8 - 3$; $2 + 3$; $5 - 0$
train 6: $7 - 1$;
$10 - 4$; $0 + 6$; $9 - 3$
train 7: $8 - 1$;
$3 + 4$; $10 - 3$; $9 - 2$

Workbook

Exercise 29

1. 5: cross out
$8 - 1$; $3 + 1$
6: cross out
$4 + 0$; $5 + 2$
7: cross out
$10 - 7$; $2 + 4$
8: cross out
$8 - 1$; $6 + 3$

(6) Interpret addition and subtraction stories

Workbook

Exercise 30

1. +; 7; 7
2. –; 3; 3
3. +; 10; 10
4. –; 4; 4
5. –; 3; 3
6. +; 4; 4

Exercise 31

1. 4 + 3 = 7; 7
2. 10 – 4 = 6; 6
3. 7 – 2 = 5; 5
4. 2 + 4 = 6; 6
5. 4 + 4 = 8; 8
6. 8 – 3 = 5; 5

Teaching activities

Tell your student a simple math story that requires addition or subtraction to solve. Use the problems in workbook exercises 30 and 31 as a guideline, or draw on real-life situations. For example:

- There were 8 dogs in our yard. 5 of them went into the neighbor's yard. How many are now in our yard?

- I saw 4 birds at our bird feeder this morning, and then I saw 2 squirrels there. How many animals did I see at the bird feeder this morning?

- There were 10 deer in the field. 7 were adults and the rest were fawns. How many fawns were there?

Ask your student to write an equation for the story. It is likely your student will be able to answer the problems easily, but writing the appropriate equation is more difficult. As numbers get larger, being able to write an equation becomes more important. If she has difficulty, provide her with counters or other objects so she can act out the story and determine whether she is finding the total or a missing part, and therefore whether to write an addition or a subtraction equation. Or, ask her to diagram the situation — circles could represent the dogs, for example.

Reinforcement

Write an addition or subtraction equation and ask your student to make up a story to go with it.

Challenge

Students often think that two numbers go on the left side of the "=" sign, with "+" or "–" between them, and the answer goes on the right side of the "=" sign. Encourage your student to understand that the "=" sign simply means that the expressions on both sides are equal by having her solve equations such as those shown below. Allow her to use counters or multilink cubes, if necessary.

$3 + 7 = 5 + \square$

$5 - 4 = 6 - \square$

$3 + 2 = 10 - \square$

$9 - \square = 3 + 3$

$4 \bigcirc 3 = 10 \bigcirc 3$

$8 \bigcirc 2 = 3 \bigcirc 3$

$5 \bigcirc 2 = 9 \bigcirc 2$

Mental Math 11

Unit 5 – Ordinal Numbers

Part 1 – Naming Positions

Ordinal numbers (first, second, third, fourth, etc.) are used to denote relative position. Your student should see the difference between ordinal numbers (1st, 2nd, 3rd, 4th, etc.) and counting, or cardinal, numbers (1, 2, 3, 4, etc.). For example, he should recognize the difference between counting out and coloring 3 items versus indicating the third or coloring the third item in a row. He also needs to know right from left, and that if we are not told which side to count from to find an item in a specified position, we start on the left (in the same direction we write or read).

There are various ways to help your student remember which side is left and which right. For example, the left hand, when held up palm outward, with the thumb at right angles to the fingers, forms the letter L, the first letter in "left". This trick, though, requires the student to remember which way a capital L goes. Or, your student could associate left or right with which hand she writes with.

You may want to teach your student to distinguish between his or her right and someone else's right.

Most children will pick up the concept of ordinal numbers used for position, particularly first, and last, but usually also second and third. "I want to be first!" "I came second." "I got the last one." Ordinal numbers are also used to indicate sequence of events, though usually not past third, or even past first, with the word "next" being used instead.

Material

Cards with the following: 1st, 2nd, 3rd, 4th, 5th, 6th, 7th, 8th, 9th, 10th (see appendix)
Ten objects that can face in a particular direction, e.g. toy animals, cars, people

(1) Name position using ordinal numbers

Teaching activities

Make sure your student knows right and left. Ask her to show you her right hand and left hand, and to point out things that are on the right or the left, from her perspective.

Set out objects, such as toy animals, people, or cars, in a row. Ask your student to imagine they are in a race and talk about which one comes in first, second, third, etc. Then set them in a line with all of them facing forward to the front of the line, and, talk about which one is first in line, second in line, etc. Ask him to point out which one is fourth, seventh, etc. Show him cards with 1st, 2nd, 3rd, 4th, ..., 10th written on them, and ask him to put them in order. Help him to read them. Pick up a card, such as 5th, and ask him to pick out the corresponding object in the line.

Now, set the objects in a line from left to right in front of your student, with them all facing the student. Point out the object farthest to the left and tell her that it is first, and ask her to find the one that is "5th from the left" etc. Point to one of the objects and ask her to tell you what position it is in, e.g., the red car is 4th from the left". Then tell her that the one farthest on the right is first, and ask her to find the object that is "2nd from the right", etc. Ask her to name the position of an object. Then, mix up the directions, e.g. "Which one is 3rd from the right? Which one is 5th from the left? The bear is third from which side? Pick out the 2nd toy from the left. Pick out 2 toys."

Tell your student that when we are not told what side to start at, we say the one to the farthest left is first.

Textbook

Page 52

Tasks 1-2, p. 53

1. B
   J
   first
2. (a) giraffe
   (b) tiger

Workbook

Exercise 32

Check answers

Exercise 33

Check answers

Exercise 34

1. 5. Check answers
6. (a)4th, 1st, 5th, 2nd, 3rd
   (b)2nd, 5th, 4th, 1st, 3rd

Reinforcement

Ask your student questions regarding position where she may need to use counters or other objects to find the answer. For example:

In a race, John is second and Mary is ninth. How many people are between John and Mary?

There is a row of children. Jasmine is fourth from the right and second from the left. How many are in the row?

Review

Before continuing on to the next unit, make sure your student knows the addition and subtraction facts through 10 well, particularly pairs of numbers that make 10.

The workbook has three review exercises in succession. You can use them as assessments to see if you need to go back and re-teach any part of units 1-5, or save them and ask your student to do several problems a day as you go on as a form of continuous review.

Workbook

Review 1
1. 7   10
2. four   two   five   ten   three
3. 6   7   4. eight   five
   9   0   5. check answers
6. 7   2
7. (a) 3 and 5   (b) 2 and 8
8. (a) 10   (b) 5
9. 9   6   0
10. draw 5 flowers
11. (a) draw 8 flowers   (b) 10

Review 2
1. 9   9   7   5
2. 3 + 2 = 5;   2 + 3 = 5;
   5 − 3 = 2;   5 − 2 = 3
3. 5   1   8   4
   10 0   9   6
   7   9
4. +; 9; 9   5. −; 5; 5
6. −; 6; 6   7. −; 6; 6
8. +; 7; 7

Review 3
1. (a) eight   (b) seven   (c) five   (d) nine
2. first set   3. second set
4. 8 → 2   4 → 6   0 → 10
5. 5th; 3rd; (1st;) 4th; 2nd
6. (a) 7   (b) 9   (c) 5   (d) 6
   (e) 6   (f) 5
7. (a) −   (b) +   (c) +   (d) −
   (e) −   (f) +   (g) −   (h) −
8. 6 + 2 = 8; 8
9. 9 − 4 = 5; 5

Unit 6 – Numbers to 20

Part 1 – Counting and Comparing

In this unit students are introduced to the base-ten system for writing numbers. We use 10 digits, 0-9. Only 1-9 are whole numbers. We can write the numerals for one through nine. To write ten, we write a 1 in the next "place" to the left. This is called the tens place, and the 1 there tells us that we have one ten. The 0 in 10 is in the ones place, and tells us there are no ones left over after the counted items are placed in groups of ten. The next number, 11, is written by starting over again with 1 in the ones place. So 11 is 1 ten and 1 one. The number in the tens place tells us how many tens (groups of ten ones) we have, and the number in the ones place tells us how many ones (groups of 1) we have. In *Primary Mathematics 2*, students will learn that 10 tens are also grouped, this time into hundreds.

Many first graders can count past ten and beyond 100 by simply counting on. Here, students will count objects up to 20 by first making a ten and then writing down the number of tens followed by the number of ones left.

In *Primary Mathematics 1B*, students will learn numbers to 100. Again, the emphasis will be on place-value, and using place-value concepts for addition and subtraction, not simply counting on.

Some students get confused which number is written first for "teen" numbers since the ones are said first, e.g. "eighteen". You can ask your student to read the number as "ten and eight" and later work on relating the number words to the numbers.

In this section, students also read and write number words. If your student's writing and spelling abilities are not up to writing number words at this time, don't require it. In places in the workbook where the student is asked to write the number in words, which requires spelling them, you can either ask him to just write the numerals, or provide the words to copy. Decide for yourself how much time you want to spend on requiring him to read the number words at this time and adjust the workbook exercises accordingly. Reading, writing, and spelling of number words can be taught apart from math lessons, and spelling number words can be taught later than reading them.

Material

Numeral cards 0-20
Number cards for 10 and ones half that size for 1-9
Number word cards, eleven to twenty
Dot cards 1-20
Counters
Multilink cubes
Playing cards 0-10

(1) Count to 20 by building up from 10

Textbook

Pages 54-55

Task 1, p. 56

1. (a) 16
   (b) 15
   (c) 18

Workbook

Exercise 35

1. 12 16 11
   17 14 15
2. 17   13
   14   20
   15   16
   11   12
3. 16   15
   14   12
   13   11

Exercise 36

1. 11; eleven
   16, sixteen
   13, thirteen
   17, seventeen
   20, twenty
2. 16 13 11
   12 20
   17 14
   19 18
   15

Teaching activities

Write the numbers 0 through 9. Tell your student that these are called "digits".

Set out 9 multilink cubes and ask your student to count them. Then add another cube and ask her how many there are. Ask her to link them together in a row. Tell her we now have a group of ten cubes in a "10-rod". Set out another cube to the right of the 10-rod, and ask your student how many there are. Write the number 11. Tell her that we write 11 as 1 group of ten, and 1 more. 10 and 1 is 11. You can show this by sliding a "1" numeral card over the "0" of a "10" card.

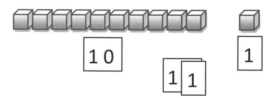

Take away the single cube and write 10 again. Lead your student to see that 10 means 1 group of 10, and 0 more. The first digit means there is 1 ten, and the second means there are no more.

Now add 2 more cubes next to the 10-rod, and ask your student to write the number. Guide him in writing a 1 for the group of ten, followed by 2 for how many more. Ask him to read the number (if necessary, he can count on from ten: eleven, twelve. 12 is read as twelve.) Tell him that twelve is 10 and 2, pointing to the digits. Use number cards for 10 and 2 and slide the 2 over the 0 of the 10.

Continue with 13, 14, 15, 16, 17, 18, and 19.

After 19, add one more and ask your student how many there are. Point out that 20 is 10 and 10 more. Tell her we write numbers as groups of ten, and have her link the ten loose cubes into a row. Write the number 20, and ask her what the first digit means (we have 2 tens). Ask her what the second digit, 0, means that there are no more than 2 groups of 10.

Show your student the number-word cards eleven through twenty, or write the number words down, and help him to read them. Ask him to match them with the number cards 11-20. Continue to provide practice in reading and writing the numbers as desired or needed.

Discuss textbook pp. 54-55 and have your student do task 1, p. 56.

Reinforcement

Say a number between 10 and 20 and ask your student to write the number and tell you the numbers as tens and ones. For example, you say "thirteen" and your student writes "13" and says "ten and three".

(2) Relate numbers from 11-19 to a ten and ones

Textbook

Tasks 2-4, pp. 57-58

2. (a) 15
   (b) 15
   (c) 15
3. (a) 14
   (b) 14
   (c) 14
4. (a) 15
   (b) 8, 18

Workbook

Exercise 37

1. (a) 16
   (b) 12
   (c) 19
   (d) 15
2. (a) 14
   (b) 18
   (c) 13
   (d) 17

Teaching activities

Draw a blank number bond. Give your student a set of objects less than 20 and have him put them in a group of ten and a group of left-overs, and then write the numbers in the number bond and as an addition equation. Repeat with other examples.

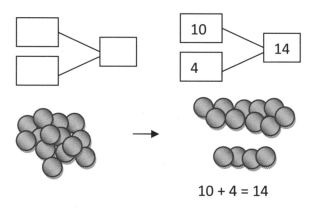

10 + 4 = 14

Have your student do tasks 2-4, textbook pp. 57-58.

Reinforcement

If needed, continue to ask your student to practice addition and subtraction facts through 10. Add the following facts:

10 + 1	10 + 2	10 + 3	10 + 4	10 + 5
10 + 6	10 + 7	10 + 8	10 + 9	
1 + 10	2 + 10	3 + 10	4 + 10	5 + 10
6 + 10	7 + 10	8 + 10	9 + 10	10 + 10

(3) Count back from 20, fill in missing numbers in a sequence

Teaching activities

Mix up a set of numeral cards 0-20 and ask your student to arrange them in order. Then have her read them from 0 to 20, and then read them backwards from 20 to 0.

Set out 20 counters. Ask your student to count them by putting them into two rows of 10. Then have her count backwards by setting one counter to the side at a time.

Set out two numeral cards that are 3 or more apart, such as 13 and 18. Ask your student to place the correct numeral cards between them: 13, 14, 15, 16, 17, 18.

Repeat, but have your student fill in the missing numbers in reverse order. For example, set out the cards 14 and 9, and ask him to put the cards 13, 12, 11, and 10 between them.

Have your student do tasks 5-6, textbook pp. 58-59.

Reinforcement

Use a set of number cards 1-20. Shuffle and place them face down. Turn over the top card and ask your student to say the numbers backwards starting with that number. Continue with the rest of the cards in the stack.

See if your student can see a pattern that skips one (odd or even numbers). Write the following patterns and ask your student to continue them.

➢ 2, 4, 6, 8, …
➢ 3, 5, 7, 9,…
➢ 20, 18, 16, 14,…
➢ 19, 17, 15, …

Textbook

Tasks 5-6, pp. 58-59

6. (a) 16, 20
   (b) 10, 11
   (c) 15, 14, 12
   (d) 8, 14
   (e) 11, 9, 7

Workbook

Exercise 38

1. picture of horse's head
2. (a) 8
   (b) 11
   (c) 14
   (d) 18

(4) Compare and order numbers within 20

Textbook

Tasks 7-11, pp. 60-61

7. B
8. A
9. (a) B   (b) C
10. (a) 17   (b) 12
11. (a) 20   (b) 8
    (c) 8, 12, 16, 20

Workbook

Exercise 39

1. (a) 8   (b) 9   (c) 4
   (d) 14   (e) 19   (f) 15
2. (a) 9   (b) 5   (c) 2
   (d) 9   (e) 8   (f) 18
3. (a) 7
   (b) 18
4. (a) 6
   (b) 14
   (c) 9
5. (a) 2, 3, 4, 5, 6 , 7, 8
   (b) 20, 19, 18, 17, 16,
       15, 14, 13
6. (a) 10, 12, 13, 15, 20
   (b) 18, 15, 14, 11, 9

Teaching activities

Set out two sets of counters with between 11 and 20 in each set. Ask your student to arrange them in tens and ones, write the number for each set, and tell you which one of the sets has the greater number and which has the smaller number.

Give your student two sets of dot cards representing two numbers between 11 and 20, such as 17 and 15, and ask your student to write the numbers for them and tell you which is the greater number and which is the smaller number. Lead her to see that if both numbers have tens, she just needs to compare the ones.

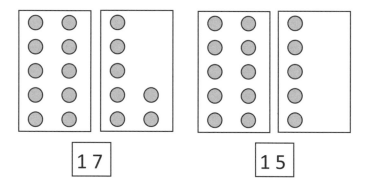

Repeat with three sets (3 numbers). Ask your student which is the greatest number and which is the smallest number. Do another example with 3 sets of dot cards, but this time include a 1-digit number.

Give your student 4 to 5 numeral cards, such as 9, 16, 20, and 11 and ask her to put them in order.

Ask your student some questions such as:

> ➢ What number is between 12 and 14?
> ➢ What number comes before 15?
> ➢ What number comes after 16?

Have your student do tasks 7-11, textbook pp. 60-61.

Reinforcement

Game
Material: 2-4 sets of numeral cards 0-20.
Procedure: Shuffle and deal all out. Each player keeps his or her cards face down. Each player turns over the top card. The player with the greatest number gets all the cards. If two players have the same number, they each turn over another card to see who wins the round.

Part 2 – Addition and Subtraction

Students should have addition and subtraction facts through 10 memorized before beginning this unit.

The following thinking strategies for addition are introduced:

➢ Make 10: Split one of the numbers up in order to make a ten with the other number (pp. 62-64)

$$8 + 5 = 10 + 3 = 13$$
$$\overset{\displaystyle /\,\backslash}{\underset{2\ \ 3}{}}$$

➢ Add the ones: To add ones to a ten and ones, add the ones (p. 65). Numbers where the sum is greater than 20 will be dealt with in *Primary Mathematics 1B*.

$$13 + 5 = 10 + 8 = 18$$
$$\overset{\displaystyle /\,\backslash}{\underset{10\ \ 3}{}}$$

➢ Subtract from the ones: To subtract ones from a ten and ones when there are enough ones, subtract the ones from the ones (pp. 65-66).

$$18 - 5 = 10 + 3 = 13$$
$$\overset{\displaystyle /\,\backslash}{\underset{10\ \ 8}{}}$$

➢ Subtract from the ten: To subtract ones from a ten and ones where there are not enough ones, subtract the ones from the tens and add that result to the ones (p. 66).

$$13 - 8 = 3 + 2 = 5$$
$$\overset{\displaystyle /\,\backslash}{\underset{3\ \ 10}{}}$$

➢ Count on: When one of the numbers is 1, 2, or 3, count on from the other number to find the answer (p. 67).

➢ Count back: When the number being subtracted is 1, 2, or 3, count back from the other number to find the answer (p. 67).

Your student should practice these strategies and should work out number facts using these strategies before memorizing them. Provide adequate concrete illustrations, particularly with the strategies of making ten and subtracting from a ten. This concept will be used many times throughout the series in a variety of contexts, and will contribute to mental math strategies for larger numbers.

After lesson 1, add the following addition facts to your fact practice and provide daily, short practice in math facts. Do not expect your student to have instant recall on these facts, but eventually she should be able to find the answers quickly, "making a ten" mentally if needed.

9 + 2	9 + 3	9 + 4	9 + 5	9 + 6	9 + 7	9 + 8	9 + 9
	8 + 3	8 + 4	8 + 5	8 + 6	8 + 7	8 + 8	8 + 9
		7 + 4	7 + 5	7 + 6	7 + 7	7 + 8	7 + 9
			6 + 5	6 + 6	6 + 7	6 + 8	6 + 9
				5 + 6	5 + 7	5 + 8	5 + 9
					4 + 7	4 + 8	4 + 9
						3 + 8	3 + 9
							2 + 9

After lesson 4, add the following subtraction facts to your daily fact practice.

11 − 10	11 − 9	11 − 8	11 − 7	11 − 6	11 − 5	11 − 4	11 − 3	11 − 2
12 − 10	12 − 9	12 − 8	12 − 7	12 − 6	12 − 5	12 − 4	12 − 3	
13 − 10	13 − 9	13 − 8	13 − 7	13 − 6	13 − 5	13 − 4		
14 − 10	14 − 9	14 − 8	14 − 7	14 − 6	14 − 5			
15 − 10	15 − 9	15 − 8	15 − 7	15 − 6				
16 − 10	16 − 9	16 − 8	16 − 7					
17 − 10	17 − 9	17 − 8						
18 − 10	18 − 9							
19 - 10								

Material

Two ten-cup egg cartons (remove the extra two cups)
Objects that fit into the egg cartons
10-frame (5 by 2 array of squares) and counters
Dot cards 1-20
Counters
Multilink cubes
Playing cards 1-10
Hundreds board
Two number cubes, labeled 5-10
Number cards 1-20
Cards with "+", "−", or "=" on them (operation cards)

(1) Add two 1-digit numbers whose sum is greater than 10 by making a 10

Textbook

Pages 62-63

Tasks 1-2, pp. 63-64

1. (a) 14   (b) 15
2. (a) 10   17
   (b) 10   14
   (c) 10   12
   (d) 10   13
   (e) 10   13

Workbook

Exercise 40

1. 13 18   2. 12 16
   16 17   13 13
   12 15   11 13
   14 11   11 15

Exercise 41

1. 12 14   2. 13 11
   15 12   11 15
   14 11   13 18
   14 12   11 11

Teaching activities

Use two 10-cup egg cartons and objects that fit into the cups as a 10-frame, or draw two 5 by 2 arrays of squares so that each square holds a counter. You can also mark off the arrays on the blank squares on the back of some laminated hundred boards.

Put 9 counters on one 10-frame and 1 on the other. Ask your student for the total, and move 1 counter over to make a ten. Say: 9 plus 1 is 10. Then put 9 counters on one frame and 2 on the other. Ask your student for the total, and move 1 counter over to make a ten. Say: 9 plus 2 is 10 and 1, or 11.

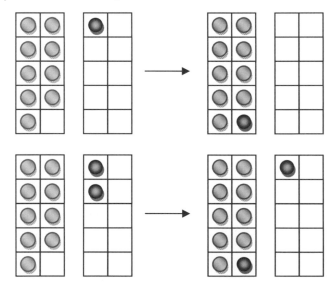

Repeat with 9 + 3. Ask your student to move counters to show other addition problems where the sum is greater than 10, such as 7 + 8 or 6 + 9. Point out that the discs do not have to be moved to the first 10-frame; in 7 + 8 they can make a ten with 8.

Then, do the same thing, but this time show the process with number bonds and write the addition equation.

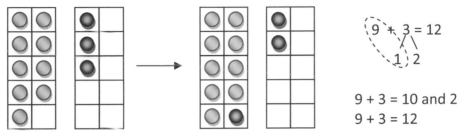

9 + 3 = 12

9 + 3 = 10 and 2
9 + 3 = 12

Discuss pages 62-63 in the textbook and have your student do tasks 1-2, pp. 63-64. Allow your student to use manipulatives for task 2, if necessary, but she should eventually answer these types of problems mentally. She should do task 2 across, rather than down first one column and then the other, to see the relationship between the two problems in each row.

Reinforcement

Rather than going on immediately to the next section in the text, spend a little time working with your student on the concept of "making a ten".

Use 10 multilink cubes stuck together in a rod, and 9 individual cubes, or a 10-rod and 9 unit cubes from a base-10 set, or any other base-10 representation, such as 10 craft sticks with a rubber band around them and 9 singles. Do not let your student break the ten down into units in the exercise that follows. If she understands that a dime is equivalent to 10 pennies, you can use 1 dime and 9 pennies.

Give your student 6 to 9 units. Then tell him a number between 5 and 9 and ask him to show you the total of the two numbers with the objects. Write the equation, e.g. 6 + 8. Since he only has a total of 9 units, he will have to use the ten to show the answer. For example, if you give him 6 units and ask him to show you 6 + 8, he will have to trade in 2 units for the ten to show 4 and 10 as the answer. Or, if you give him 9 units and ask him to show you 9 + 7, he will have to trade in 3 units for the ten to show you 10 and 6 as the answer.

Write some problems in the following format, and ask your student to fill in the blanks:

➢ 9 + 5 = 10 + _____
➢ 4 + 7 = 10 + _____

If your student has trouble with these, discuss the number bond that can be formed with one of the numbers to make a ten with the other number.

You can ask your student to memorize doubles. He should already know:

1 + 1 = 2	2 + 2 = 4	3 + 3 = 6
4 + 4 = 8	5 + 5 = 10	

Have your student learn the following doubles:

6 + 6 = 12	7 + 7 = 14
8 + 8 = 16	9 + 9 = 18

Then, you can use dot cards to show another strategy for adding two numbers that differ by 1, or "doubles + 1".

6 + 7 = 12 + 1 = 13
7 + 8 = 14 + 1 = 15
8 + 9 = 16 + 1 = 17

Your student can use either method (doubles + 1 or making a ten) to find the answers to these.

Games

Material: Playing cards, with face cards removed. The Ace is 1.
Procedure: Play a game similar to "War". Shuffle and deal all cards out. Each player turns over two cards and adds the numbers on their card. The player with the highest total gets all the cards. After all cards have been turned over, the player with the most cards wins.

Material: Two number cubes labeled 5-10, counters, a game-board with the numbers 10-20 written randomly on a grid (You can use as large a grid as you like. For example, use a wet-erase marker and write the numbers 10 to 20 randomly in the blank squares on the back of a laminated hundreds board.)
Procedure: Players take turns throwing the number cube, adding the numbers, and putting their counter on the answer on the game board. The first player to get three counters in a line (vertically, horizontally, or diagonally) wins.

Mental Math 12-14

(2) Add a 1-digit number to a 2-digit number within 20 by adding ones

Teaching activities

Use two 10-frames and counters.

Write an addition expression where a 1-digit number is added to a 2-digit number with a sum within 20, such as 12 + 6. Have him place 12 counters on the ten-frame and 6 by themselves. Then have him add the 6 to the ten-frame and tell you the answer to the expression. Repeat with some other examples. Then, do the same thing but show the process with a number bond and write the equation. Point out that we can think of the 2-digit number as ten and ones, and add the ones together. We will then have the ten and the total ones for the answer.

Textbook

Tasks 3-4, p. 65

3. 17
4. (a) 19, 19
   (b) 20, 20

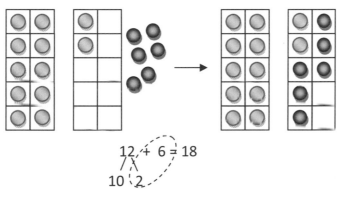

12 + 6 = 18
10 2

12 + 6 = 10 and 8   12 + 6 = 18

Do a few problems where adding the ones make another ten, such as 13 + 7. Ask your student to add the tens, and then realize that she now has 2 tens, so the answer is 20.

13 + 7 = 20
10 3

13 + 7 = 10 and 10
13 + 7 = 20

Have your student do tasks 3-4, textbook p. 65.

Reinforcement

Mental Math 15

Workbook

Exercise 42

1. 15   19
   17   18
   19   18
   20   19
2. 19   18
   20   16
   17   18
   17   17
3. 20   6; 17
   4; 16   5; 15
   8; 19   4; 14
   3; 17   5; 18

(3) Subtract a 1-digit number from a 2-digit number by subtracting ones

Textbook

Tasks 5-6, pp. 65-66

5. 12
6. (a) 15   (b) 12

Workbook

Exercise 43

1. 12   10
   13   12
   13   10
   13   14
2. 12   11
   12   17
   12   11
   13   15
3. 11   3; 14
   2; 10   7; 10
   3; 10   2; 12
   10; 10   4; 12

Teaching activities

Use two 10-frames and counters, as in the previous activities, or a 10-rod of multilink cubes and ones.

Write a subtraction expression where a 1-digit number is subtracted from a 2-digit number where the ones is greater than the ones being subtracted, such as 18 – 6. Illustrate the first number with the 10-frames and counters, or multilink cubes. Ask your student to take away the second number. It should be obvious that she needs to simply take away the correct number of ones. Illustrate a few other examples, and then include a drawing of a number bond, showing the first number as 10 and ones, and the second number being subtracted from the ones.

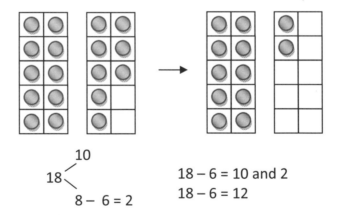

18 – 6 = 10 and 2
18 – 6 = 12

Write some similar subtraction problems and see if your student can find the answer. Draw a number bond if needed. Only use subtraction situations where there are enough ones to take away from. Include an example where all the ones are subtracted, e.g. 13 – 3. In each case, point out that there are enough ones to subtract from.

$$19 - 5 = 14$$
$$/ \backslash$$
$$10 \quad 9$$

$$17 - 3 = 14$$
$$/ \backslash$$
$$10 \quad 7$$

$$13 - 3 = 10$$
$$/ \backslash$$
$$10 \quad 3$$

$$15 - 5 = 10$$
$$/ \backslash$$
$$10 \quad 5$$

Only use subtraction situations where there are enough ones to take away from. Include an example where all the ones are subtracted, e.g. 13 – 3.

Write the expression 20 – 10 and ask your student to solve. There are 2 tens, take away 1 ten, that leaves 1 ten. 20 – 10 = 10.

Have your student do tasks 5-6, textbook pp. 65-66.

Reinforcement

Mental Math 16

(4) Subtract from a 2-digit number by subtracting from a ten

Textbook

Tasks 7-8, p. 66

7. 8
8. (a) 5, 6, 9
   (b) 4, 5, 8

Workbook

Exercise 44

1. 5	6
4	2
5	7
10	2
2. 6	5
8	2
4	8
6	7
3. 9	7
7	9
8	8
7	9

Teaching activities

Use two 10-frames and counters.

Write a subtraction expression where a 1-digit number is subtracted from a 2-digit number when the ones is smaller than the ones being subtracted, e.g. 15 – 7. Show the first number on the ten-frames. Tell your student that he can solve this problem using facts he already knows. 10 – 7 = 3. Remove 7 from the full 10-frame. This leaves 3. Ask your student for the total amount left. There are 3 + 5 = 8 left. So, 15 – 7 = 8.

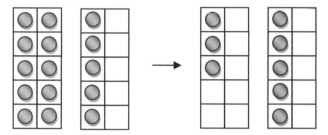

$$15 - 7 = 8$$

Now, show the same process with 13 – 6, but this time also draw a number bond to show that we are subtracting from a ten.

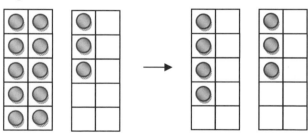

$$10 - 6 = 4$$
$$13 \diagdown$$
$$3$$

13 – 6 = 4 and 3
13 – 6 = 7

Repeat with other examples, eventually just drawing the number bond and not using manipulatives.

Have your student do tasks 7-8, textbook p. 66. Allow your student to use the 10-rod and the 9 ones for task 8. She cannot take the 10-rod apart to find the answer.

Remind your student that in subtraction, we are finding a missing part.
Write the equations

$$13 - 6 = \underline{\quad}$$
$$6 + \underline{\quad} = 13$$

Tell your student that she can find the missing part by thinking of how many more are needed to make 10 with 6 (4) and then add on the remaining 3. (4 + 3 = 7)

Write the expression 20 – 10 and ask your student to solve it. There are 2 tens, take away 1 ten, that leaves 1 ten. 20 – 10 = 10.

Write some problems involving subtracting from 20, e.g. 20 – 4. Show that we can subtract from a ten. If we know that 10 – 4 = 6, then we know that 20 – 4 = 10 and 6, or 16.

$$10 - 4 = 6$$
$$20 \diagdown$$
$$10$$

20 – 4 = 10 and 6
20 – 4 = 16

Give your student a 10-rod of multilink cubes and 9 unit cubes. Tell him the 10-rod cannot come apart. Ask him to show you the answer to some problems such as 14 – 8. He first shows 14 with a ten and 4 ones. Then he must take away 8. To do this, he will have to trade in the 10-rod for 2 ones.

Reinforcement

Provide plenty of additional practice in subtraction problems involving taking away from the ten.

If your student has a lot of difficulty with the concept, or with going from using manipulatives to finding the answer mentally, you can teach another strategy:

13 – 6: First take away 3 from the ten. That is not taking away enough. We need to take away another 3 (since 6 – 3 = 3). Essentially, we are doing the subtraction in two steps:

13 – 6: 13 – 3 = 10, 10 – 3 = 7

Repeat with some other examples, e.g:

17 – 9: Take away 7 to get down to 10, need to take away another 2 to take away 9 in all, the answer is 8.

Write some problems in the following format, and ask your student to fill in the blanks:

$$13 - 6 = \underline{\hspace{1cm}} + 3$$
$$14 - 7 = 3 + \underline{\hspace{1cm}}$$

If your student understands that a dime is worth the same as 10 pennies, you can illustrate subtracting from a ten as making change. Give him a dime and 5 pennies. Say: You have a dime and 5 pennies. You want to buy something that costs 7 pennies. How can you pay for it? 5 pennies are not enough, so you have to pay with the dime. How much change do you get? 3 pennies. How much money do you now have? 3 pennies from the change and 5 pennies you still have is 8 pennies. 15 – 7 = 8.
Ask your student to make change for other similar situations.

Practice:
Use playing cards with face cards removed.
Shuffle cards and place all face-down.
Select a target number, such as 14, and write it down.
Turn over the cards one at a time, and ask your student to subtract the card from the target number and give the answer.
After a while, change the target number.

Mental Math 17-19

(5) Add or subtract 1, 2, or 3 by counting on or back

Teaching activities

Write the numbers 1 to 20 in a row, or ask your student to lay out the number cards 1 to 20 in a row.

Point to a number and ask your student to add or subtract 1, 2, or 3 from it by counting up or down. For example, point to 11 and say "subtract 3". Ask her to count down: 10, 9, 8. Make sure she does not use the number that you are pointing at as one of the numbers that is being added or subtracted.

Then, ask your student to do the same thing without a number line. Write down a number within 20 and tell him to add or subtract 1, 2, or 3. For example, write down 11 and tell him to add 2.

Have your student do tasks 9-12, textbook p. 67.

Reinforcement

Continue to ask your student to practice addition and subtraction, using fact cards, games, and activities from previous lessons.

Mental Math 20

Textbook

Tasks 9-12, p. 67

9. 11
10. (a) 11 (b) 12
    (c) 16 (d) 19
11. 9
12. (a) 8 (b) 9
    (c) 13 (d) 16

Workbook

Exercise 45

1. 11, 13, 20, 14, 19, 12
   15, 18, 14, 20, 16, 19
   14, 18, 12, 20, 16, 13
   15, 19, 11, 17, 13, 10
   16, 13, 19, 14, 17, 11
   8, 17, 14, 9, 18, 11
2. 18, 19, 17, 17, 16
   18, 19, 19,
   17, 17, 16, 18,
   19, 19, 17, 19, 19, 18
   20

(6) Add and subtract within 20

Workbook

Exercise 46

1. (down)
      12 8   7   11
      15 5 16 3
2. 11 6   8
      12 6   8
       6 12 9
      12 13

Exercise 47

Check answers

Exercise 48

1. –   +
   +   –
   +   +
   –   –
   –   +
2. $8 + 4 = 12$ or $4 + 8 = 12$
   $9 + 5 = 14$ or $5 + 9 = 14$
   $16 - 9 = 7$ or $16 - 7 = 9$
   $13 - 5 = 8$ or $13 - 8 = 5$
3. $7 + 6 = 13$ $13 - 6 = 7$
   $6 + 7 = 13$ $13 - 7 = 6$
   $11 + 5 = 16$ $16 - 5 = 11$
   $5 + 11 = 16$ $16 - 11 = 5$

Exercise 49

1. $18 - 13 = 5$ $13 - 5 = 8$
   $3 + 6 = 9$ $9 + 0 = 9$
   $11 + 9 = 20$ $9 + 9 = 18$
   $16 - 10 = 6$ $20 - 17 = 3$
   $4 + 6 = 10$

Teaching activities

Show your student two sets of counters or multilink cubes, using different colors. For example, set out 5 blue counters and 7 red ones. Guide your student in writing two addition and two related subtraction problems for the situation.

$7 + 5 = 12$ $5 + 7 = 12$
$12 - 7 = 5$ $12 - 5 = 7$

Write some addition and subtraction equations without the plus or minus sign, and ask your student to fill in the symbols. For example:

$18 \bigcirc 5 = 13$
$5 \bigcirc 6 = 11$

Give your student some number cards and cards with the plus, minus, and equal sign on them and ask him to form an equation.

Tell your student some simple word problems involving addition or subtraction within 20 and have her write the expression that would be used to solve the problem and find the answer.

Reinforcement

Write the following and ask your student to solve:

13 + 7 = 5 + ☐

15 – 8 = 17 – ☐

9 + 5 = 20 – ☐

14 ◯ 3 = 10 ◯ 1

18 ◯ 2 = 15 ◯ 5

Mental Math 21-22

Review

Workbook

Review 4

1. (a) 9   (b) 8
   (c) 11   (d) 12
   (e) 14   (f) 18
   (g) 20   (h) 17
2. $6 + 7 = 13 = 10 + 3$ $9 + 3 = 12 = 10 + 2$
   $8 + 8 = 16 = 10 + 6$ $7 + 7 = 14 = 10 + 4$
3. $8 + 6 = 14$ $14 - 8 = 6$
   $6 + 8 = 14$ $14 - 6 = 8$
4. (a) 10, 11, 12, 13, 14, 15, 16,17,18, 20
   (b) 20, 19, 18, 17, 16, 15, 14, 13, 12, 11
5. (a) 19   (b) 9
6. (a) draw 12   (b) 13
7. 1st   3rd   2nd   4th
8. H
9. (a) 10   (b) 8   (c) 0   (d) 10
10. $14 + 5 = 19$;   19
11. $12 - 4 = 8$;   8

Review 5

1. (a) 15   (b) 20
2. (a) 10   (b) 5   (c) 10   (d) 2
3. (a) 12   (b) 19   (c) 14   (d) 16
4. (a) B   (b) C
5. (a) 13   (b) 4
6. (a) 10; 11; 12   (b) 2; 3; 4
7. (a) 7   (b) 11
8. (a) 19; 15; 0; 6
   (b) 6; 4; 10; 14
9. $12 - 5 = 7$; 7
10. $14 + 3 = 17$; 17
11. $15 - 8 = 7$; 7

The workbook has 2 review exercises in succession. You can use them as assessments to see if you need to go back and re-teach any part of units 1-6, or save them and ask your student to do several problems a day as you go on as a form of continuous review.

Mental Math 23-24

Unit 7 – Shapes

Part 1 – Common Shapes

The emphasis in this unit is on practical work. Students need to know the names of the shapes for circle, square, rectangle, and triangle. At this stage, you can have your student regard squares as different shapes than rectangles. In the *Primary Mathematics* curriculum, students are not required to use the words cube, cone, sphere, cylinder, etc. It is up to you if you want to teach your student these terms. Use real objects or photos rather than 2-dimensional drawings of 3-dimensional shapes.

Students will be sorting objects by shape, size, or color. Sorting objects by shapes requires the student to pay attention to number of sides and corners.

Students will be identifying and continuing patterns based on shape, size, color, or orientation. Some students can see patterns, such as those on p. 75 of the text, easier when they verbalize them. Ask your student to "say" the pattern, e.g. rectangle, circle, triangle, rectangle, circle, triangle, … or upright, sideways, upright, …. At this stage only one or two attributes (out of shape, size, color, or position) change. For example, the pattern in (d) changes by position and color, but shape and size stays the same.

Material

3-dimensional models of cubes, rectangular and triangular prisms, cylinders, cones, and pyramids
Attribute blocks or cutouts of 3 different sizes each of rectangles, squares, circles, and triangles in 3 or 4 colors
Pattern blocks or a set of 4-5 cutouts each of 4-5 different shapes
Shape stickers, if available

(1) Identify common shapes

Textbook

Page 68

Task 1, pp. 69-70

Workbook

Exercise 50

1. check answers
2. shape that should be colored:
   Third; Third; Second
   First; Second
3. rectangle, circle, triangle, circle, rectangle

Exercise 51

1. square
   triangle
   circle,
   rectangle
   rectangle
2. (a) square
   (b) circle
   (c) circle
   (d) triangle
   (e) square
   (f) rectangle
   (g) triangle
   (h) triangle

Teaching activities

Give your student some 3-dimensional models and discuss their shapes and characteristics, e.g., number of faces, edges, and corners, whether they roll or not, whether they can be stacked or not. Extend the discussion to similar objects around the room, e.g. tin cans, rolling pin, balls, boxes, dice, etc.

Draw a circle, triangle, square, and rectangle. Label each and make sure your student knows the names of these four shapes. Ask her to describe features of the shapes. Some shapes have no corners; others have sharp corners and flat sides. Ask her to count the number of corners and sides of these four shapes. Tell her that a square is just like a rectangle, but all its sides are equal in length.

Discuss p. 68 in the textbook. Ask your student to talk about the different types of building blocks and shapes that children in the picture could trace from the faces. Then ask him to trace the faces of the 3-dimensional models onto paper. Ask him to name the faces she has traced on the paper.

Have your student do task 1, textbook pp. 69-70.

Reinforcement

Ask your student to draw a picture consisting of the various shapes put together, such as a picture of a robot.

Teaching activities

Give your student some attribute blocks or cutouts of different sizes and colors of circles, rectangles, squares, and triangles and ask him to sort them in different ways. He could sort by shape, by size, by number of edges, or by color. You can discuss sub-groups as well. For example, he could first sort the shapes into those with no corners or those with corners, then sort the shapes with corners into shapes with 3 corners and shapes with 4 corners, and then sort the shapes with 4 corners into rectangles and squares. You can draw a tree diagram of the different categories, for example:

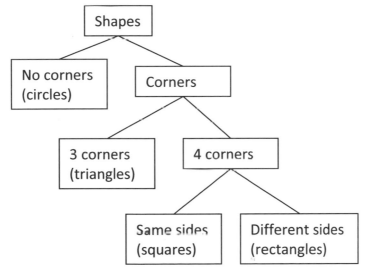

Discuss task 2, textbook pp. 71-73.

Extension

Ask your student to sort shapes that are not similar, such as different types of triangles (right, acute, or obtuse triangles) and different shapes of rectangles (tall and thin, short and fat, etc.).

Discuss and sort other shapes, such as ovals, parallelograms, trapezoids, or hexagons.

Textbook

Task 2, pp. 71-73

Workbook

Exercise 52

Check answers

Exercise 53

Check answers

(3) Identify patterns

Textbook

Tasks 3-4, pp. 74-75

3. (a) same shape, different size
   (b) different shape, different size
   (c) same shape and size
   (d) same shape and size
4. (a) triangle
   (b) small red triangle
   (c) a rectangle on its side
   (d) blue upside triangle pointing down

Workbook

Exercise 54

1. (a)   circle
   (b)   rectangle
   (c)   smaller square
   (d)   rectangle
   (e)   triangle
2. row 2: square, rectangle
   row 3: rectangle, circle, triangle, square
   row 4: triangle, rectangle

Teaching activities

Draw or use cut-out shapes to show two shapes that have the same shape and color but different size. Ask your student to identify similarities and differences between them.

Repeat with other pairs of shapes that differ by one attribute, such as same shape and size but different color. Include examples where the pair only differs in orientation.

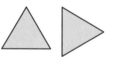

Now show pairs of shapes where two of the attributes are different, such as size and shape.

Discuss task 3, textbook p. 74. Ask your student to explain how the two cutout shapes differ.

Draw or use cut-out shapes or pattern blocks to display a sequence of shapes. Ask your student to read the pattern out loud to determine what comes next in the pattern. For example:

Triangle, triangle, square, triangle, triangle, square…

Ask your student to draw boxes or circles around the repeated patterns.

Ask your student to do task 4, textbook p. 75. Get your student to read the pattern aloud and find out what comes next.

Reinforcement

Ask your student to look for patterns in the environment.

Ask your student to create patterns with stickers or pattern blocks.

(4) Combine shapes

Textbook

Tasks 5-7, pp. 76-77

5. Pink with red, orange with blue, purple with green
6. Blue with green, pink with purple

Workbook

Exercise 55

Check answers.

Teaching activities

Ahead of time, put some pattern blocks or cut-out shapes together and trace the outline. Then ask your student to use a selection of shapes and try to find out which shapes were used to make the outline.

Cut some basic shapes into two parts in various ways, mix them up, and ask your student to try to pair them up to make the original shapes (see p. 76 of the textbook).

Have your student do tasks 5-7, textbook pp. 76-77.

Reinforcement

Ask your student to put a jigsaw puzzle together.

Unit 8 – Length

Part 1 – Comparing Length

Students should already be familiar with terms such as tall, short, long, and with terms dealing with comparison such as shorter than and longer than. They should know the difference between size and length, and between length and height.

Students will compare length in a variety of ways:

> Physical appearance: One object is obviously longer than another (pp. 78-79).

> Direct comparison: Please the objects side by side and have the same starting point (this is actually an important concept in model drawing, which will come later).

> Counting identical units: Compare the length by comparing the number of units (pp. 80-81).

> Measure using non-standard units: Place a set of identical units end to end to match the length of each object, and then count the number of units to compare (pp. 82-83).

> Using paper tape to represent each length: Cut a paper tape to represent the length of one object and compare it with the length of another object, or cut a paper tape for each object and compare them.

Give your student concrete experience with each of these methods – don't just have her look at the pictures in the textbook.

Material

Multilink cubes
Paper or cardboard strips

(1) Compare length

Textbook

Pages 78-79

Tasks 1-4, pp. 80-81

1. The green string is longest.
   The yellow string is shortest.
2. The blue block is tallest.
   The yellow block is shortest.
3. C-worm takes the longest path.
   B-worm takes the shortest path.
4. R-tape is the longest
   Q-tape is the shortest.

Workbook

Exercise 56

Check answers.

Exercise 57

1. (a) C
   (b) B
   (c) A
   (d) C
2. C; B; D; A

Teaching activities

Put multilink cubes into rods of 4 lengths, 2 of which are the same, and ask your student to compare their lengths. Ask your student to line them up and say sentences such as:
"The red one is as long as the blue one."
"The yellow one is longer than the red one."
"The yellow one is the longest."
"The green one is the shortest."

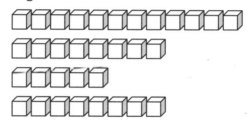

Then ask your student how she would compare the lengths if the rods were not placed side by side. Since the cubes are all of the same length, the lengths can be compared by counting the cubes. Have her count the cubes and compare the lengths.

Put two objects of different but similar length at different places in the room. Ask your student how he could find out which one is longer if he cannot move them next to each other. Allow him to carry out his ideas. Give him a paper strip and lead him to see that he can use a third object that is longer than both, mark off the length of each on the strip, and compare the marks.

Discuss pages 78-79 in the textbook and have your student do tasks 1-4, pp. 80-81.

Reinforcement

Compare lengths or heights of items in the environment throughout the day.

Part 2 – Measuring Length

In this section, students will measure lengths using non-standard units such as paper clips, multilink cubes, and craft sticks. The standard units (e.g. centimeter, meter, inch, foot, yard) will be introduced in *Primary Mathematics 2*.

To measure the object, the student will place the units end to end alongside the objects to match the length. They should see that it is not always possible to have an exact number of units to match the length. Use the word "about" to express the result of an approximate measurement.

Encourage your student to estimate a length before measuring it.

Material

Multilink cubes
Paper clips (2 different sizes)

(1) Estimate and measure length

Textbook

Page 82

Tasks 1-2, pp. 82-83

Workbook

Exercise 58

1. 7
   7
   5
   7
2. 5
   6
   12
3. middle one
4. (a) 7
   (b) 5
   (c) 3

Teaching activities

Ask your student to measure an object with a chain of paper clips. Since the length will probably not end at exactly the end of a paper clip, discuss approximate lengths using the term "about". An object that is a bit more than 8 paper clips long is about 8 paper clips long, whereas one that is a bit less than 9 paper clips long is about 9 paper clips long. Write down the length, along with the unit, e.g. about 8 paper clips.

Then ask your student to measure the same object with a different unit, such as a chain of larger paper clips. Write down the length along with the unit, e.g. about 9 short paper clips and about 5 large paper clips.

Discuss the difference in numerical value for the lengths. The length of an object will have different values when it is measured with different units. Lead your student to see that an object's length will have a larger value when measured with a smaller unit.
Ask your student to measure the length of another object with the paper clips. Then ask him if the number of the length will be greater or smaller with the second type of unit.

Ask your student to estimate the length of a third object in both types of measuring units, and then measure their lengths.

Discuss p. 82 of the text.

Have your student do tasks 1-2, pp. 82-83.

Reinforcement

Let your student compare the lengths or heights of various objects in the environment using chains of paper clips.

Start a growth chart on a wall to measure the student's height over time.

Measure the growth of a plant using non-standards units, such as paper clips. You can extend the paper-clip chain as the plant grows.

Unit 9 – Weight

Part 1 – Comparing Weight

Weight, like length and shape, is also an attribute of an object. Students are generally already familiar with the terms heavy, light, lighter, etc. used when comparing weight.

Weight can be compared in a variety of ways.

➢ Use the objects' "heft": When two objects are obviously different we can compare them by heft or lifting (p. 84).

➢ Direct comparison: Place objects on each side of a balance. The heavier one makes the balance on its side go down farther (pp. 85).

➢ Measure using non-standard units: Use identical units to balance each object one at a time on the balance. Then compare the number of units needed (p. 86).

➢ If one object weighs the same as a second object, we can measure the weight of a third object with the second object to compare its weight with the first object.

Again, give your students concrete experience. If you don't have a balance, you can build a simple one. Tape a ruler to the table so that it sticks out perpendicularly with a side. Hang a coat hanger on the ruler. Hang some paper cups from each side of the coat hanger. Encourage your student to estimate the weight when weighing with non-standard units.

Technically, weight is the measure of the gravitational pull between two objects, and mass is the measure of how much matter, or inertia, an object has. An object on the moon has the same mass as it has on earth, but it weighs less. When we use a balance to compare two objects, we are actually comparing their mass. When we use a scale, we are measuring the weight. Since the term weight is used more commonly for both, you can use that term for both weight and mass until your student learns the difference in science studies.

Material

3-4 objects of similar weight
Simple balance
Clay or Play-dough
Multilink cubes
Marbles, counters, or other objects that can be used as unit weights

(1) Compare weight

Textbook

Pages 84-85

Tasks 1-3, pp. 85-86

1. (a) the ruler
   (b) the key
2. 5

Workbook

Exercise 59

1. (a) as heavy as
   (b) heavier than
   (c) lighter than

Teaching activities

Ask your student to compare the weight of several objects of obviously different weights, using terms such as lighter, heavier, lightest, heaviest, as light as, as heavy as, same weight.

Use three or more objects that are similar in weight, such as a pear, an apple, and a banana, and ask your student how we could compare their weights. Show him a balance and have him use that to compare the weights of the objects and put them in order of weight. The objects have to be compared in pairs.

Ask your student how we could compare objects that we cannot put together on the balance, for some reason. Lead her to see that we can compare the weight to something that we could change to match, such as clay. Give her two objects and have her use clay to match the weight of one, and then compare the second object to the weight of the clay.

Lead your student to see that we could also use a set of identical units to balance each object, and then compare the number of units needed. Ask him to use multilink cubes to balance several objects, and then compare the weight of those objects by the number of multilink cubes needed.

Reinforcement

Young children often relate weight to size. Use some objects where the larger object is lighter than the smaller object and ask your student to compare their weights.

Part 2 – Measuring Weight

In this section, students will measure weight using non-standard units such as multilink cubes, counters, or marbles. The standard units (e.g. gram, kilogram, pound, ounce) will be introduced in *Primary Mathematics 2*.

Depending on the accuracy of your balance and the weight of the units, it may not always be possible to have an exact number of units to match the weight of an object. If one more object makes the balance dip more on the side with the units, you can say the weight of the object is "about" or "almost" the same as the number of units.

Encourage your student to estimate the weight of an object before measuring it.

Material

3-4 objects of similar weight
Simple balance
Multilink cubes
Marbles, counters, or other objects that can be used as unit weights

(1) Estimate and measure weight

Textbook

Page 87

Tasks 1-2, p. 88

1. Box A = 6 units
   Box B =8 units
   Box C = 7 units
   Box B is heaviest,
   Box A is lightest.

Workbook

Exercise 60

1. (a) 7
   (b) 9
   (c) 3
2. (a) 5
   (b) 4

Exercise 61

1. (a) 7
   (b) 9
   (c) 8
   (d) watermelon
   (e) papaya
   (f) watermelon
2. (a) 6
   (b) 11
   (c) 5
   (d) C
   (e) C
   (f) B

Teaching activities

Ask your student to measure the weight of an object with a balance using multilink cubes as the unit. Then ask her to weigh the same object with a different unit, such as counters. Write down the weights, along with the unit, e.g. 8 multilink cubes, 15 counters. Discuss the difference in numerical value for the weights. Ask your student to compare the weight of the units and lead her to see that it takes more of the lighter unit to weigh the object than of the heavier unit.

Ask your student to estimate the weight of other objects in various units, and then weigh them and record their weight in various units.

Discuss textbook p. 87 and have your student do tasks 1-2, p. 88.

Extension

Students do not learn about standard units of weight at this level, but many have experience with hearing that their weight is so many pound or kilograms. If you have pound or kilogram weights, you can introduce them informally, and ask your student to weigh various things using the pound or kilogram as the unit, and compare to their own weight. They could also weigh themselves and other things on a bathroom scale.

Review

Workbook

Review 6

1. 12   11
   16   17
2. 13   19
   11   12
   20   15
   16   14
3. (a) 17   (b) 7
4. $14 - 6 = 8 = 4 + 4$ $12 - 3 = 9 = 7 + 2$
   $15 - 8 = 7 = 2 + 5$ $14 - 9 = 5 = 1 + 4$
5. the last triangle
6. (a) R; Q   (b) C; B; C
7. $19 - 5 = 14$; 14
8. $12 - 8 = 4$; 4
9. $8 + 7 = 15$; 15

Review 7

1. (a) twelve   (b) twenty
2. (a) 3 watermelons colored (b) 3rd pineapple colored
3. 3, 6, 7, 11, 14
4. (a) 12   (b) 3
5. (a) 13   (b) 5
6. (a) 9   (b) 1
   (c) 10   (d) 8
   (e) 16   (f) 13
   (g) 14   (h) 9
7. (a) A; E   (b) C   (c) B
8. the last figure
9. the first and last figure
10. $10 - 6 = 4$; 4
11. $14 - 7 = 7$; 7
12. $16 - 9 = 7$; 7

Mental Math 1	Mental Math 2	Mental Math 3
5 + 0 = **5**	4 + 2 = **6**	6 + 1 = **7**
1 + 4 = **5**	6 + 3 = **9**	2 + 4 = **6**
5 + 1 = **6**	3 + 5 = **8**	1 + 8 = **9**
7 + 1 = **8**	1 + 9 = **10**	7 + 3 = **10**
3 + 2 = **5**	2 + 5 = **7**	2 + 8 = **10**
1 + 2 = **3**	7 + 1 = **8**	3 + 5 = **8**
0 + 4 = **4**	5 + 3 = **8**	9 + 1 = **10**
2 + 3 = **5**	2 + 7 = **9**	5 + 2 = **7**
1 + 5 = **6**	3 + 4 = **7**	3 + 6 = **9**
2 + 2 = **4**	3 + 7 = **10**	7 + 2 = **9**
9 + 0 = **9**	1 + 6 = **7**	4 + 3 = **7**
4 + 1 = **5**	6 + 2 = **8**	1 + 7 = **8**
1 + 6 = **7**	3 + 3 = **6**	2 + 3 = **5**
8 + 1 = **9**	8 + 2 = **10**	6 + 3 = **9**
2 + 2 = **4**	3 + 2 = **5**	2 + 6 = **8**
0 + 8 = **8**	3 + 6 = **9**	3 + 3 = **6**
6 + 1 = **7**	4 + 3 = **7**	2 + 7 = **9**
1 + 7 = **8**	7 + 2 = **9**	5 + 3 = **8**
9 + 0 = **9**	8 + 1 = **9**	3 + 4 = **7**
2 + 1 = **3**	5 + 2 = **7**	8 + 2 = **10**

Mental Math 4	Mental Math 5	Mental Math 6
1 + 1 = **2**	8 + 2 = **10**	5 − 1 = **4**
3 + 2 = **5**	4 + 5 = **9**	4 − 3 = **1**
6 + 2 = **8**	1 + 1 = **2**	3 − 3 = **0**
3 + 3 = **6**	3 + 4 = **7**	4 − 1 = **3**
3 + 7 = **10**	5 + 5 = **10**	2 − 0 = **2**
2 + 8 = **10**	6 + 4 = **10**	2 − 1 = **1**
4 + 6 = **10**	0 + 6 = **6**	1 − 0 = **1**
5 + 4 = **9**	8 + 2 = **10**	5 − 4 = **1**
3 + 4 = **7**	4 + 3 = **7**	4 − 2 = **2**
2 + 2 = **4**	2 + 3 = **5**	2 − 2 = **0**
0 + 8 = **8**	7 + 3 = **10**	5 − 5 = **0**
9 + 1 = **10**	4 + 4 = **8**	3 − 0 = **3**
4 + 5 = **9**	3 + 5 = **8**	4 − 4 = **0**
5 + 3 = **8**	1 + 9 = **10**	5 − 3 = **2**
4 + 4 = **8**	5 + 4 = **9**	3 − 2 = **1**
4 + 6 = **10**	2 + 8 = **10**	5 − 0 = **5**
6 + 3 = **9**	3 + 6 = **9**	3 − 1 = **2**
5 + 5 = **10**	2 + 7 = **9**	1 − 1 = **0**
7 + 0 = **7**	3 + 3 = **6**	4 − 0 = **4**
7 + 2 = **9**	3 + 6 = **9**	5 − 2 = **3**

Mental Math 7	Mental Math 8	Mental Math 9
6 − 1 = **5**	8 − 6 = **2**	7 − 4 = **3**
5 − 2 = **3**	10 − 4 = **6**	8 − 4 = **4**
7 − 1 = **6**	6 − 4 = **2**	3 − 2 = **1**
5 − 3 = **2**	10 − 1 = **9**	10 − 7 = **3**
9 − 1 = **8**	10 − 9 = **1**	10 − 8 = **2**
10 − 2 = **8**	8 − 7 = **1**	8 − 5 = **3**
8 − 2 = **6**	10 − 5 = **5**	9 − 4 = **5**
10 − 1 = **9**	9 − 7 = **2**	6 − 6 = **0**
9 − 2 = **7**	7 − 6 = **1**	9 − 6 = **3**
6 − 2 = **4**	10 − 2 = **8**	7 − 4 = **3**
7 − 3 = **4**	9 − 8 = **1**	6 − 3 = **3**
8 − 3 = **5**	10 − 9 = **1**	9 − 5 = **4**
7 − 2 = **5**	6 − 5 = **1**	8 − 5 = **3**
4 − 3 = **1**	10 − 3 = **7**	5 − 2 = **3**
9 − 3 = **6**	5 − 4 = **1**	10 − 4 = **6**
7 − 3 = **4**	10 − 10 = **0**	9 − 6 = **3**
6 − 3 = **3**	10 − 6 = **4**	10 − 5 = **5**
8 − 1 = **7**	5 − 3 = **2**	9 − 5 = **4**
8 − 3 = **5**	10 − 7 = **3**	10 − 6 = **4**
10 − 3 = **7**	4 − 3 = **1**	7 − 3 = **4**

Mental Math 10	Mental Math 11
4 + 5 = **9**	10 − 1 = 4 + **5**
7 − 4 = **3**	10 − 4 = 9 − **3**
9 − 3 = **6**	6 − 4 = 10 − **8**
5 + 2 = **7**	10 − 3 = 3 + **4**
8 − 4 = **4**	10 − 9 = 1 + **0**
6 + 2 = **8**	8 − 7 = 9 − **8**
10 − 7 = **3**	10 − 5 = 3 + **2**
9 − 4 = **5**	9 − 2 = 4 + **3**
4 + 5 = **9**	7 − 5 = 10 − **8**
8 − 5 = **3**	10 − 2 = 5 + **3**
3 + 4 = **7**	9 − 8 = 5 − **4**
7 − 5 = **2**	4 + 1 = 9 − **4**
9 − 5 = **4**	8 − 5 = 10 − **7**
4 + 4 = **8**	8 − 3 = 2 + **3**
9 − 6 = **3**	1 + 1 = 7 − **5**
10 − 4 = **6**	10 − 4 = 9 − **3**
6 − 3 = **3**	9 − 0 = 6 + **3**
8 + 2 = **10**	5 − 3 = 8 − **6**
8 − 3 = **5**	10 − 7 = 2 + **1**
7 + 3 = **10**	4 − 1 = 7 − **4**

Mental Math 12	Mental Math 13
9 + 1 = 10 + **0**	7 + 4 = 10 + **1**
9 + 2 = 10 + **1**	4 + 8 = 10 + **2**
7 + 3 = 10 + **0**	9 + 7 = 10 + **6**
8 + 6 = 10 + **4**	7 + 5 = 10 + **2**
9 + 9 = 10 + **8**	8 + 5 = 10 + **3**
6 + 5 = 10 + **1**	7 + 9 = 10 + **6**
8 + 3 = 10 + **1**	6 + 4 = 10 + **0**
5 + 5 = 10 + **0**	9 + 3 = 10 + **2**
9 + 5 = 10 + **4**	8 + 2 = 10 + **0**
8 + 4 = 10 + **2**	7 + 6 = 10 + **3**
6 + 6 = 10 + **2**	8 + 4 = 10 + **2**
5 + 7 = 10 + **2**	6 + 7 = 10 + **3**
3 + 8 = 10 + **1**	2 + 9 = 10 + **1**
2 + 9 = 10 + **1**	7 + 8 = 10 + **5**
4 + 7 = 10 + **1**	9 + 6 = 10 + **5**
7 + 7 = 10 + **4**	6 + 8 = 10 + **4**
5 + 8 = 10 + **3**	5 + 6 = 10 + **1**
9 + 6 = 10 + **5**	8 + 8 = 10 + **6**
3 + 9 = 10 + **2**	6 + 9 = 10 + **5**
8 + 7 = 10 + **5**	5 + 9 = 10 + **4**

Mental Math 14	Mental Math 15	Mental Math 16
8 + 3 = **11**	3 + 4 = **7**	7 − 4 = **3**
9 + 6 = **15**	13 + 4 = **17**	17 − 4 = **13**
5 + 7 = **12**	4 + 13 = **17**	6 − 3 = **3**
9 + 2 = **11**	8 + 1 = **9**	16 − 3 = **13**
6 + 8 = **14**	18 + 1 = **19**	15 − 2 = **13**
8 + 8 = **16**	8 + 11 = **19**	18 − 5 = **13**
7 + 6 = **13**	5 + 4 = **9**	19 − 6 = **13**
3 + 9 = **12**	15 + 4 = **19**	19 − 2 = **17**
8 + 5 = **13**	5 + 14 = **19**	18 − 4 = **14**
7 + 9 = **16**	17 + 2 = **19**	13 − 2 = **11**
5 + 6 = **11**	14 + 4 = **18**	18 − 5 = **13**
9 + 9 = **18**	5 + 12 = **17**	19 − 4 = **15**
4 + 8 = **12**	11 + 7 = **18**	16 − 6 = **10**
8 + 9 = **17**	3 + 10 = **13**	17 − 3 = **14**
6 + 6 = **12**	16 + 2 = **18**	18 − 6 = **12**
7 + 7 = **14**	12 + 3 = **15**	17 − 4 = **13**
9 + 4 = **13**	13 + 5 = **18**	19 − 5 = **14**
4 + 7 = **11**	2 + 12 = **14**	16 − 4 = **12**
8 + 7 = **15**	1 + 12 = **13**	20 − 6 = **14**
5 + 9 = **14**	10 + 8 = **18**	13 − 3 = **10**

Mental Math 17	Mental Math 18
12 − 10 = 0 + **2**	11 − 9 = **2**
12 − 9 = 1 + **2**	12 − 4 = **8**
12 − 8 = 2 + **2**	14 − 6 = **8**
12 − 6 = 4 + **2**	13 − 7 = **6**
12 − 9 = **1** + 2	11 − 5 = **6**
12 − 8 = **2** + 2	14 − 9 = **5**
14 − 8 = 2 + **4**	12 − 9 = **3**
14 − 6 = 4 + **4**	13 − 5 = **8**
13 − 7 = 3 + **3**	15 − 8 = **7**
12 − 5 = **5** + 2	12 − 8 = **4**
17 − 9 = **1** + 7	16 − 7 = **9**
15 − 7 = **3** + 5	11 − 6 = **5**
16 − 9 = **1** + 6	13 − 4 = **9**
14 − 8 = **2** + 4	17 − 9 = **8**
11 − 4 = **6** + 1	14 − 5 = **9**
12 − 3 = **7** + 2	11 − 2 = **9**
13 − 6 = **4** + 3	20 − 7 = **13**
20 − 9 = 10 + **1**	12 − 5 = **7**
20 − 6 = 10 + **4**	16 − 6 = **10**
20 − 3 = **10** + 7	20 − 4 = **16**

Mental Math 19	Mental Math 20	Mental Math 21
12 − 7 = **5**	9 + 2 = **11**	12 − 4 = **8**
15 − 6 = **9**	15 − 3 = **12**	16 − 8 = **8**
16 − 9 = **7**	11 − 3 = **8**	9 + 9 = **18**
11 − 8 = **3**	13 + 2 = **15**	11 − 2 = **9**
13 − 9 = **4**	20 − 2 = **18**	8 + 7 = **15**
20 − 4 = **16**	12 + 3 = **15**	13 − 8 = **5**
12 − 3 = **9**	13 − 2 = **11**	5 + 9 = **14**
16 − 8 = **8**	16 − 1 = **15**	18 − 9 = **9**
11 − 7 = **4**	8 + 3 = **11**	12 − 8 = **4**
18 − 8 = **10**	11 − 2 = **9**	6 + 7 = **13**
13 − 8 = **5**	14 + 1 = **15**	8 − 3 = **5**
14 − 7 = **7**	12 − 3 = **9**	13 − 4 = **9**
12 − 6 = **6**	14 − 3 = **11**	5 + 5 = **10**
17 − 8 = **9**	9 + 3 = **12**	14 − 7 = **7**
11 − 4 = **7**	19 − 2 = **17**	12 − 9 = **3**
14 − 8 = **6**	12 − 2 = **10**	4 + 8 = **12**
15 − 7 = **8**	20 − 1 = **19**	15 − 7 = **8**
11 − 3 = **8**	16 + 2 = **18**	19 − 5 = **14**
13 − 6 = **7**	20 − 3 = **17**	10 − 6 = **4**
20 − 5 = **15**	17 + 3 = **20**	11 − 6 = **5**

Mental Math 22	Mental Math 23	Mental Math 24
11 − 3 = **8**	13 − 6 = **7**	15 − 6 = **9**
14 − 8 = **6**	3 + 9 = **12**	8 + 5 = **13**
9 + 4 = **13**	14 − 5 = **9**	7 + 7 = **14**
8 + 8 = **16**	7 + 9 = **16**	11 − 9 = **2**
12 − 3 = **9**	2 + 8 = **10**	14 − 6 = **8**
9 + 8 = **17**	11 − 4 = **7**	16 − 4 = **12**
13 − 5 = **8**	6 + 6 = **12**	9 + 6 = **15**
16 − 9 = **7**	14 − 9 = **5**	12 − 5 = **7**
14 + 3 = **17**	10 − 8 = **2**	9 + 2 = **11**
17 − 5 = **12**	6 + 8 = **14**	17 − 9 = **8**
11 − 7 = **4**	17 − 8 = **9**	3 + 3 = **6**
6 + 2 = **8**	20 − 7 = **13**	11 − 5 = **6**
15 − 8 = **7**	11 − 8 = **3**	5 + 6 = **11**
8 + 3 = **11**	7 + 4 = **11**	3 + 7 = **10**
13 − 9 = **4**	15 − 5 = **10**	15 + 5 = **20**
5 + 7 = **12**	12 − 6 = **6**	13 − 7 = **6**
9 − 3 = **6**	15 − 9 = **6**	20 + 0 = **20**
7 + 2 = **9**	5 + 4 = **9**	13 + 4 = **17**
12 + 8 = **20**	11 + 9 = **20**	20 − 2 = **18**
12 − 7 = **5**	12 − 2 = **10**	16 − 7 = **9**

Mental Math 1	Mental Math 2	Mental Math 3
5 + 0 = _____	4 + 2 = _____	6 + 1 = _____
1 + 4 = _____	6 + 3 = _____	2 + 4 = _____
5 + 1 = _____	3 + 5 = _____	1 + 8 = _____
7 + 1 = _____	1 + 9 = _____	7 + 3 = _____
3 + 2 = _____	2 + 5 = _____	2 + 8 = _____
1 + 2 = _____	7 + 1 = _____	3 + 5 = _____
0 + 4 = _____	5 + 3 = _____	9 + 1 = _____
2 + 3 = _____	2 + 7 = _____	5 + 2 = _____
1 + 5 = _____	3 + 4 = _____	3 + 6 = _____
2 + 2 = _____	3 + 7 = _____	7 + 2 = _____
9 + 0 = _____	1 + 6 = _____	4 + 3 = _____
4 + 1 = _____	6 + 2 = _____	1 + 7 = _____
1 + 6 = _____	3 + 3 = _____	2 + 3 = _____
8 + 1 = _____	8 + 2 = _____	6 + 3 = _____
2 + 2 = _____	3 + 2 = _____	2 + 6 = _____
0 + 8 = _____	3 + 6 = _____	3 + 3 = _____
6 + 1 = _____	4 + 3 = _____	2 + 7 = _____
1 + 7 = _____	7 + 2 = _____	5 + 3 = _____
9 + 0 = _____	8 + 1 = _____	3 + 4 = _____
2 + 1 = _____	5 + 2 = _____	8 + 2 = _____

Mental Math 4	Mental Math 5	Mental Math 6
$1 + 1 =$ _____	$8 + 2 =$ _____	$5 - 1 =$ _____
$3 + 2 =$ _____	$4 + 5 =$ _____	$4 - 3 =$ _____
$6 + 2 =$ _____	$1 + 1 =$ _____	$3 - 3 =$ _____
$3 + 3 =$ _____	$3 + 4 =$ _____	$4 - 1 =$ _____
$3 + 7 =$ _____	$5 + 5 =$ _____	$2 - 0 =$ _____
$2 + 8 =$ _____	$6 + 4 =$ _____	$2 - 1 =$ _____
$4 + 6 =$ _____	$0 + 6 =$ _____	$1 - 0 =$ _____
$5 + 4 =$ _____	$8 + 2 =$ _____	$5 - 4 =$ _____
$3 + 4 =$ _____	$4 + 3 =$ _____	$4 - 2 =$ _____
$2 + 2 =$ _____	$2 + 3 =$ _____	$2 - 2 =$ _____
$0 + 8 =$ _____	$7 + 3 =$ _____	$5 - 5 =$ _____
$9 + 1 =$ _____	$4 + 4 =$ _____	$3 - 0 =$ _____
$4 + 5 =$ _____	$3 + 5 =$ _____	$4 - 4 =$ _____
$5 + 3 =$ _____	$1 + 9 =$ _____	$5 - 3 =$ _____
$4 + 4 =$ _____	$5 + 4 =$ _____	$3 - 2 =$ _____
$4 + 6 =$ _____	$2 + 8 =$ _____	$5 - 0 =$ _____
$6 + 3 =$ _____	$3 + 6 =$ _____	$3 - 1 =$ _____
$5 + 5 =$ _____	$2 + 7 =$ _____	$1 - 1 =$ _____
$7 + 0 =$ _____	$3 + 3 =$ _____	$4 - 0 =$ _____
$7 + 2 =$ _____	$3 + 6 =$ _____	$5 - 2 =$ _____

Mental Math 7	Mental Math 8	Mental Math 9
6 − 1 = _____	8 − 6 = _____	7 − 4 = _____
5 − 2 = _____	10 − 4 = _____	8 − 4 = _____
7 − 1 = _____	6 − 4 = _____	3 − 2 = _____
5 − 3 = _____	10 − 1 = _____	10 − 7 = _____
9 − 1 = _____	10 − 9 = _____	10 − 8 = _____
10 − 2 = _____	8 − 7 = _____	8 − 5 = _____
8 − 2 = _____	10 − 5 = _____	9 − 4 = _____
10 − 1 = _____	9 − 7 = _____	6 − 6 = _____
9 − 2 = _____	7 − 6 = _____	9 − 6 = _____
6 − 2 = _____	10 − 2 = _____	7 − 4 = _____
7 − 3 = _____	9 − 8 = _____	6 − 3 = _____
8 − 3 = _____	10 − 9 = _____	9 − 5 = _____
7 − 2 = _____	6 − 5 = _____	8 − 5 = _____
4 − 3 = _____	10 − 3 = _____	5 − 2 − _____
9 − 3 = _____	5 − 4 = _____	10 − 4 = _____
7 − 3 = _____	10 − 10 = _____	9 − 6 = _____
6 − 3 = _____	10 − 6 = _____	10 − 5 = _____
8 − 1 = _____	5 − 3 = _____	9 − 5 = _____
8 − 3 = _____	10 − 7 = _____	10 − 6 = _____
10 − 3 = _____	4 − 3 = _____	7 − 3 = _____

Mental Math 10	Mental Math 11
$4 + 5 =$ _____	$10 - 1 = 4 +$ _____
$7 - 4 =$ _____	$10 - 4 = 9 -$ _____
$9 - 3 =$ _____	$6 - 4 = 10 -$ _____
$5 + 2 =$ _____	$10 - 3 = 3 +$ _____
$8 - 4 =$ _____	$10 - 9 = 1 +$ _____
$6 + 2 =$ _____	$8 - 7 = 9 -$ _____
$10 - 7 =$ _____	$10 - 5 = 3 +$ _____
$9 - 4 =$ _____	$9 - 2 = 4 +$ _____
$4 + 5 =$ _____	$7 - 5 = 10 -$ _____
$8 - 5 =$ _____	$10 - 2 = 5 +$ _____
$3 + 4 =$ _____	$9 - 8 = 5 -$ _____
$7 - 5 =$ _____	$4 + 1 = 9 -$ _____
$9 - 5 =$ _____	$8 - 5 = 10 -$ _____
$4 + 4 =$ _____	$8 - 3 = 2 +$ _____
$9 - 6 =$ _____	$1 + 1 = 7 -$ _____
$10 - 4 =$ _____	$10 - 4 = 9 -$ _____
$6 - 3 =$ _____	$9 - 0 = 6 +$ _____
$8 + 2 =$ _____	$5 - 3 = 8 -$ _____
$8 - 3 =$ _____	$10 - 7 = 2 +$ _____
$7 + 3 =$ _____	$4 - 1 = 7 -$ _____

Mental Math 12	Mental Math 13
9 + 1 = 10 + _____	7 + 4 = 10 + _____
9 + 2 = 10 + _____	4 + 8 = 10 + _____
7 + 3 = 10 + _____	9 + 7 = 10 + _____
8 + 6 = 10 + _____	7 + 5 = 10 + _____
9 + 9 = 10 + _____	8 + 5 = 10 + _____
6 + 5 = 10 + _____	7 + 9 = 10 + _____
8 + 3 = 10 + _____	6 + 4 = 10 + _____
5 + 5 = 10 + _____	9 + 3 = 10 + _____
9 + 5 = 10 + _____	8 + 2 = 10 + _____
8 + 4 = 10 + _____	7 + 6 = 10 + _____
6 + 6 = 10 + _____	8 + 4 = 10 + _____
5 + 7 = 10 + _____	6 + 7 = 10 + _____
3 + 8 = 10 + _____	2 + 9 = 10 + _____
2 + 9 = 10 + _____	7 + 8 = 10 + _____
4 + 7 = 10 + _____	9 + 6 = 10 + _____
7 + 7 = 10 + _____	6 + 8 = 10 + _____
5 + 8 = 10 + _____	5 + 6 = 10 + _____
9 + 6 = 10 + _____	8 + 8 = 10 + _____
3 + 9 = 10 + _____	6 + 9 = 10 + _____
8 + 7 = 10 + _____	5 + 9 = 10 + _____

Mental Math 14	Mental Math 15	Mental Math 16
8 + 3 = _____	3 + 4 = _____	7 − 4 = _____
9 + 6 = _____	13 + 4 = _____	17 − 4 = _____
5 + 7 = _____	4 + 13 = _____	6 − 3 = _____
9 + 2 = _____	8 + 1 = _____	16 − 3 = _____
6 + 8 = _____	18 + 1 = _____	15 − 2 = _____
8 + 8 = _____	8 + 11 = _____	18 − 5 = _____
7 + 6 = _____	5 + 4 = _____	19 − 6 = _____
3 + 9 = _____	15 + 4 = _____	19 − 2 = _____
8 + 5 = _____	5 + 14 = _____	18 − 4 = _____
7 + 9 = _____	17 + 2 = _____	13 − 2 = _____
5 + 6 = _____	14 + 4 = _____	18 − 5 = _____
9 + 9 = _____	5 + 12 = _____	19 − 4 = _____
4 + 8 = _____	11 + 7 = _____	16 − 6 = _____
8 + 9 = _____	3 + 10 = _____	17 − 3 = _____
6 + 6 = _____	16 + 2 = _____	18 − 6 = _____
7 + 7 = _____	12 + 3 = _____	17 − 4 = _____
9 + 4 = _____	13 + 5 = _____	19 − 5 = _____
4 + 7 = _____	2 + 12 = _____	16 − 4 = _____
8 + 7 = _____	1 + 12 = _____	20 − 6 = _____
5 + 9 = _____	10 + 8 = _____	13 − 3 = _____

Mental Math 17	Mental Math 18
$12 - 10 = 0 +$ _____	$11 - 9 =$ _____
$12 - 9 = 1 +$ _____	$12 - 4 =$ _____
$12 - 8 = 2 +$ _____	$14 - 6 =$ _____
$12 - 6 = 4 +$ _____	$13 - 7 =$ _____
$12 - 9 =$ _____ $+ 2$	$11 - 5 =$ _____
$12 - 8 =$ _____ $+ 2$	$14 - 9 =$ _____
$14 - 8 = 2 +$ _____	$12 - 9 =$ _____
$14 - 6 = 4 +$ _____	$13 - 5 =$ _____
$13 - 7 = 3 +$ _____	$15 - 8 =$ _____
$12 - 5 =$ _____ $+ 2$	$12 - 8 =$ _____
$17 - 9 =$ _____ $+ 7$	$16 - 7 =$ _____
$15 - 7 =$ _____ $+ 5$	$11 - 6 =$ _____
$16 - 9 =$ _____ $+ 6$	$13 - 4 =$ _____
$14 - 8 =$ _____ $+ 4$	$17 - 9 =$ _____
$11 - 4 =$ _____ $+ 1$	$14 - 5 =$ _____
$12 - 3 =$ _____ $+ 2$	$11 - 2 =$ _____
$13 - 6 =$ _____ $+ 3$	$20 - 7 =$ _____
$20 - 9 = 10 +$ _____	$12 - 5 =$ _____
$20 - 6 = 10 +$ _____	$16 - 6 =$ _____
$20 - 3 =$ _____ $+ 7$	$20 - 4 =$ _____

Mental Math 19	Mental Math 20	Mental Math 21
12 − 7 = _____	9 + 2 = _____	12 − 4 = _____
15 − 6 = _____	15 − 3 = _____	16 − 8 = _____
16 − 9 = _____	11 − 3 = _____	9 + 9 = _____
11 − 8 = _____	13 + 2 = _____	11 − 2 = _____
13 − 9 = _____	20 − 2 = _____	8 + 7 = _____
20 − 4 = _____	12 + 3 = _____	13 − 8 = _____
12 − 3 = _____	13 − 2 = _____	5 + 9 = _____
16 − 8 = _____	16 − 1 = _____	18 − 9 = _____
11 − 7 = _____	8 + 3 = _____	12 − 8 = _____
18 − 8 = _____	11 − 2 = _____	6 + 7 = _____
13 − 8 = _____	14 + 1 = _____	8 − 3 = _____
14 − 7 = _____	12 − 3 = _____	13 − 4 = _____
12 − 6 = _____	14 − 3 = _____	5 + 5 = _____
17 − 8 = _____	9 + 3 = _____	14 − 7 = _____
11 − 4 = _____	19 − 2 = _____	12 − 9 = _____
14 − 8 = _____	12 − 2 = _____	4 + 8 = _____
15 − 7 = _____	20 − 1 = _____	15 − 7 = _____
11 − 3 = _____	16 + 2 = _____	19 − 5 = _____
13 − 6 = _____	20 − 3 = _____	10 − 6 = _____
20 − 5 = _____	17 + 3 = _____	11 − 6 = _____

Mental Math 22	Mental Math 23	Mental Math 24
11 − 3 = _____	13 − 6 = _____	15 − 6 = _____
14 − 8 = _____	3 + 9 = _____	8 + 5 = _____
9 + 4 = _____	14 − 5 = _____	7 + 7 = _____
8 + 8 = _____	7 + 9 = _____	11 − 9 = _____
12 − 3 = _____	2 + 8 = _____	14 − 6 = _____
9 + 8 = _____	11 − 4 = _____	16 − 4 = _____
13 − 5 = _____	6 + 6 = _____	9 + 6 = _____
16 − 9 = _____	14 − 9 = _____	12 − 5 = _____
14 + 3 = _____	10 − 8 = _____	9 + 2 = _____
17 − 5 = _____	6 + 8 = _____	17 − 9 = _____
11 − 7 = _____	17 − 8 = _____	3 + 3 = _____
6 + 2 = _____	20 − 7 = _____	11 − 5 = _____
15 − 8 = _____	11 − 8 = _____	5 + 6 = _____
8 + 3 = _____	7 + 4 = _____	3 + 7 = _____
13 − 9 = _____	15 − 5 = _____	15 + 5 = _____
5 + 7 = _____	12 − 6 = _____	13 − 7 = _____
9 − 3 = _____	15 − 9 = _____	20 + 0 = _____
7 + 2 = _____	5 + 4 = _____	13 + 4 = _____
12 + 8 = _____	11 + 9 = _____	20 − 2 = _____
12 − 7 = _____	12 − 2 = _____	16 − 7 = _____

0   1   2

3   4   5

6   7   8

9	10	11
12	13	14
15	16	17

18 19 20

one two

three four

five six

seven

eight

nine

ten

eleven

twelve

thirteen

fourteen

fifteen

sixteen

seventeen

eighteen

nineteen

twenty

zero

1st | 2nd | 3rd

4th | 5th | 6th

7th | 8th | 9th

1 0 10th

+ - =

+ - =

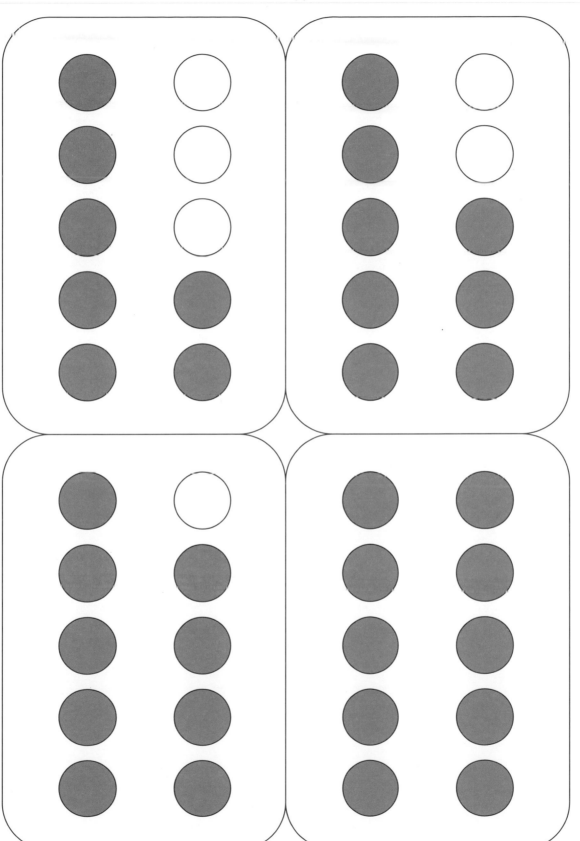

1	2	3	4	5	6	7	8	9	10
11	12	13	14	15	16	17	18	19	20
21	22	23	24	25	26	27	28	29	30
31	32	33	34	35	36	37	38	39	40
41	42	43	44	45	46	47	48	49	50
51	52	53	54	55	56	57	58	59	60
61	62	63	64	65	66	67	68	69	70
71	72	73	74	75	76	77	78	79	80
81	82	83	84	85	86	87	88	89	90
91	92	93	94	95	96	97	98	99	100